Alleluia America!

Alleluia America!

An Irish Journalist in Bush Country

Carole Coleman

The Liffey Press

Published by
The Liffey Press
Ashbrook House
10 Main Street, Raheny,
Dublin 5, Ireland
www.theliffeypress.com

A catalogue record of this book is
available from the British Library.

ISBN 1-904148-76-X

Illustrations © Jeanette Dunne

Printed in Spain by Graficas Cems.

Contents

About the Author

Carole Coleman is from Carrick-on-Shannon, County Leitrim. She has worked as a journalist for almost two decades, both in Ireland and the US. In 1993 she joined RTÉ and served as Washington Correspondent from 2000 to 2004. This is her first book.

Acknowledgements

Sincere thanks are due to David Givens of The Liffey Press for the opportunity to write this book and to Liffey's senior editor Brian Langan for his judicious work. Thanks also to the tireless Heidi Murphy. I am truly grateful to Jeanette Dunne for her illustrations and to Sinead McKenna of Sin É Design for the cover. I am also indebted to agent Jonathan Williams, to Ed Mulhall of RTÉ and to Ray Kennedy for their keen eyes. Thanks to all the Colemans and Larry Schott for everything else.

Chapter 1

Let Me Finish

"OH, ANGEL OF GOD, my guardian dear, to whom God's love commits me here. Ever this day, be at my side, to light, to guard, to rule and guide. Amen."

I stared at the mirror in the ladies' powder room and recited the shortest prayer I knew. When I was finished, Stephanie, my producer, began a prayer aloud. It too was brief and in Hebrew. I had no idea what it meant but it had a very reassuring sound. I touched up my makeup and opened the door that led directly back into the Vermeil Room. This room is a rich yellow and is decorated with arrangements of fresh-cut flowers. Around its walls are portraits of former First Ladies. There is an elegant Jackie Kennedy in a silvery evening gown and Nancy Reagan in shimmering red. Lady Bird Johnson had posed in a stylish yellow gown and Eleanor Roosevelt appeared stern in a grey suit.

I don't know if Stephanie and I were heard praying aloud in the White House bathroom but our handlers looked at us as though they suspected a political coup had been plotted in there.

"Is everything OK?" asked MC, the White House press officer.

"Yes, fine," I assured her, trying to ignore the dull nervous pain starting to pulse in my right hand.

"The President has been briefed. He will be down shortly."

MC, AS SHE IS KNOWN around the White House, had phoned me three days earlier to say that President George W. Bush would do an interview with RTÉ. "Good news," she had said. "It goes this Thursday at 4.20 pm. You will have ten minutes with the President and Turkish television will talk to him just before you." After weeks of speculating on the likelihood of an interview to coincide with his visit to Ireland, which was now just four days away, my reaction was one of sweet relief. It was over a year into the invasion of Iraq, and Ireland currently held the rotating Presidency of the European Union. I knew that this visit was the best chance I would ever have of getting to interview George Bush.

My initial excitement was dampened only by the timing, which was much later than I had hoped. The interview would take place just three hours before I was to fly back to Ireland to cover his arrival at the EU Summit at Dromoland Castle in County Clare and just fifteen minutes before the start of RTÉ's *Prime Time* programme where the interview would be broadcast. It would be practically impossible to have the President on air in time for this.

"That's just fabulous," I gushed, "but is there any way I could go before the Turks?" I had previously explained about the *Prime Time* programme, so MC knew the situation. "I'll look into it," she offered helpfully.

Conducting the interview sounded like quite a production. We wouldn't be able to just saunter in there with a camera. It would be filmed by a White House crew, which would then hand over the tapes to me to be copied and returned to them the same day.

MC had also asked me for a list of questions and topics, which she said was required for policy purposes in case I should want to ask something which the President needed to be briefed on. The request did not seem odd to me then. The drill had been exactly the same for an interview I had conducted six months earlier with then Secretary of State Colin Powell.

"What would you ask the President of the United States?" I enquired of everyone I met in the following days. Ideas had already been scribbled on scattered notepads in my bedroom, on scraps of paper in my handbag and on my desk, but once the date was confirmed, I mined suggestions from my peers in RTÉ and from foreign policy analysts. I grilled my friends in Washington and even pestered the cab drivers. I had everyone around me annoyed.

"What would you ask?"

"I'd ask him when he's leaving," was the most popular suggestion in the nation's capital. After turning all this over in my head, I settled on a list of ten questions.

Skirt or trouser suit was the next decision. I had been working in television long enough to know that men, with all that gravitas, could get away with almost anything, while women were expected to look like fashion models as well as ask intelligent questions. A new suit would have to be altered and there wasn't time for that. Most of my skirts were above the knee, which would be sure to attract comments from the Irish viewing public, so I chose the deep red trouser suit I had worn when I interviewed for the job of RTÉ's Washington Correspondent almost four years earlier. It still looked smart and it was comfortable. Besides, I had come to look on it as my "lucky suit".

WITH MOST TELEVISION EVENTS the logistics take up a great deal of the reporter's time and energy, and this event was as complicated as it gets. Securing a time swap with Turkish television would ensure that I saw the President ten minutes earlier than originally scheduled but there was still less than half an hour to bring the taped interview from the White House to the production place four blocks away in time for the *Prime Time* special. There would be no time to edit the three-camera shoot that the White House was planning. On such a shoot, one camera is trained on the President, a second on the interviewer, while a third films the "two-shot" of both participants from a side angle. For broadcast, these tapes have to be alternated or "switched" to make the scene look natural. We would have to switch it as the interview played out live to Dublin, a highly skilled job requiring a director. RTÉ had flown one of its top directors in from Dublin to do the job.

I also had to plan a quick getaway from the White House. All visitors have to be escorted in and out and often you might have to hang around until someone becomes available. MC offered the services of an agile intern, a marathon runner who, we were told, would be assigned to escort us out without delay. Producer Stephanie Sweiki and I timed the run from the White House to the production studio. We could dash across Lafayette Park, dodge through traffic for a few blocks up to 16th Street, cut right for one more block and reach our destination in less than four minutes, without high heels!

With the arrangements falling into place, the sense of chaos receded and I returned to the questions, which by now were perpetually dancing around my head, even in my sleep. Reporters often begin a big interview by asking a soft question — to let the subject warm up before getting into the substance of the topic at hand. This was how I had initially intended to begin with Mr Bush but, as I mentally rehearsed the likely scenario, I felt that too much time could be consumed by the President's first probable answer, praising Ireland and looking forward to his visit . . . and so on. We could, I had calculated, be into the third minute before even getting to the controversial topics. I decided to ditch the cordial introduction. The majority of the Irish public, as far as I could tell, was angry with George Bush and did not want to hear a cosy fireside chat in the middle of the most disputed war since

Vietnam. Instead of the kid glove start, I would get straight down to business.

WHEN THURSDAY 24 JUNE rolled around, Washington DC was bathed in a moist ninety-degree heat, the type that makes you perspire all over after you have walked just two blocks. The city is built on swampland and in the summer months is one of the most humid spots in America.

I got my hair done, donned the red suit and slipped on an opal ring that had belonged to my maternal grandmother, Rebecca. Before setting off for the White House, I phoned home to Carrick-on-Shannon for my mother's pep talk. No one can do pep talks like Kathleen Coleman. "Now don't be afraid to speak up", she would say, or "Remember to sit straight and don't be slouching". But she and my father had gone to Enniskillen for the day and I had to make do without her words of wisdom.

Stephanie and I arrived at the north-west gate of the White House that afternoon to find the interviewer from Turkish television there before us, along with his producer. We were directed to the Old Executive Office building, Vice President Dick Cheney's headquarters, for the ritual identification and screening, and were then introduced to MC, whom I had spoken to only by phone. An elegant and confident woman, she was the cut of CJ, the feisty White House press secretary on the *West Wing* television drama. A younger male sidekick named Colby stood close by nodding at everything she said and interjecting with a few comments of his own every now and then. "Anyone for a Coke?" MC asked as we sat in her office reviewing the procedure for the interview. With the heat and the anticipation, everyone was parched.

We left the Old Executive Office building by the back, cut across the parking lot and entered the White House through a staff door. Inside, we followed a long shiny corridor to the Library. The White House Library is a mid-sized room with grey panelling, a fireplace and bookshelves, a place where past presidents liked to

conduct less formal meetings. It was already set up for our interview with cameras, monitors and a maze of wires criss-crossing
the floor. I stared at the two chairs by the fireplace where the
President and I were to sit. They were at least six feet apart; clearly
I would not be getting too close to him. From the Library we were
led to the Vermeil Room to wait.

As the nerves crept up on me, I paced about. There was some
small talk about Bertie Ahern and just as I was mentally tuning out
from the general chit-chat to rehearse my questions one last time,
sidekick Colby suggested that I ask the President about the yellow
suit the Taoiseach had worn the previous week at the G8 Summit
on Sea Island in Georgia. I laughed loudly and then stopped to
study his face for signs that he was joking — but he didn't appear to
be. "The President has a good comment on that," he said. The
Taoiseach's suit had been a shade of cream, according to the Irish
Embassy. But alongside the other more conservatively dressed
leaders, it had appeared as a bright yellow, leaving our Bertie looking more like the lead singer in a band than the official representa-
tive of the European Union. It was amusing at the time but I was
not about to raise a yellow suit with the President. "Really?" I asked
politely. But a little red flag went up inside my head.

For me nervousness manifests itself as a dull tingling pain in
my right hand just between the thumb and forefinger. It had begun on the day I sat the first paper of my Leaving Cert examina-
tion and since then has reappeared selectively on bumpy flights
and as a prelude to important events. I was feeling it when MC
announced that she had some news for me. "There may be another
interview in the pipeline for you," she said.

"Me?"

"We're not supposed to tell you this yet, but we are trying to set
up an interview with the First Lady." She indicated that the White
House had already been in contact with RTÉ to make arrangements for the interview at Dromoland Castle, where the President
and Mrs Bush would be staying. As an admirer of Laura Bush's

cool grace and sharp intellect, I had requested interviews with her several times previously without any reply. Now the First Lady of the United States was being handed to me on a plate. I could not believe my luck.

"Of course, it's not certain yet," MC added.

And then her sidekick dropped his second bombshell.

"We'll see how you get on with the President first."

I'm sure I continued smiling, but I was stunned. What I understood from this was that if I pleased the White House with my questioning of the President, I would get to interview the First Lady. Were they trying to ensure a soft ride for the President, or was I the new flavour of the month with the first family? My hand was fairly throbbing now.

"I'm going to give the President his final briefing. Are there any further questions you want to pass on to him?" MC asked.

"No," I said, "just tell him I want to chat."

It was at this point that Stephanie and I locked eyes and headed for the ladies' powder room where we prayed.

WITH JUST MINUTES TO GO, I was escorted to the Library where a staff member gave instructions on how to greet the President.

"He'll be coming in the door behind you, just stand up, turn around and extend your hand." I placed my notes on the coffee table, someone attached a microphone to my lapel, and I sat and waited. The room was now well lit, providing the kind of warm background conducive to a fireside chat. Several people had crowded in behind me. I counted five members of the White House film crew, there was a White House stenographer sitting in the corner and three or four security staff standing around motionless. I was still counting them when someone spoke.

"He's coming."

I stood up, turned around to face the door and seconds later the President of the United States strode in towards me.

George W. Bush appeared shorter than on camera and he looked stern and rather grey that day.

"Thanks for comin', Mr President!" I said as I stuck out my hand to him.

I had borrowed this greeting directly from him. When George Bush made a speech at a rally or town hall, he always began by saying "Thanks for comin'" in his man-of-the-people manner. If he detected the humour in my greeting, he didn't let on. He took my hand with a firm grip and, bringing his face right up close to mine, stared me straight in the eyes for several seconds, as though drinking in every detail of my face. He sat down and an aide attached a microphone to the inside of his jacket. Nobody said a word. "We don't address the President unless he speaks first," a member of the film crew had told me earlier. The resulting silence seemed odd and discomforting to me, so I broke it.

"How has your day been, Mr President?"

Without looking up at me, he continued to straighten his tie and replied in a strong Texan drawl, "Very busy."

This was followed by an even more disconcerting silence which, compounded by the six feet separating us, made it difficult to establish any rapport.

"Will Mrs Bush be seeing any of our beautiful country?" I tried again, attempting to warm things up by adding that I had heard that the Taoiseach would be keeping him too busy for sightseeing.

"He's putting me to work, is he? Have you not interviewed Laura?"

"No, I haven't met your wife." Mindful of the conversation with the handlers, I suggested that he put in a good word for me. He chuckled. By now he seemed settled and the crew looked ready but still nobody spoke. There didn't seem to be anyone firing a starting gun and I was beginning to worry that the clock may have already started on my ten minutes.

"Are we all ready to go then?" I asked, looking around the room. The next voice I heard was the President's.

"I think we have a spunky one here," he said, to no one in particular.

"MR PRESIDENT," I BEGAN. "You will arrive in Ireland in less than twenty-four hours' time. While our political leaders will welcome you, unfortunately the majority of our people will not. They are annoyed about the war in Iraq and about Abu Ghraib. Are you bothered by what Irish people think?" The Abu Ghraib prisoner abuse scandal was making news then, generating a lot of negative attention for America and the Bush administration.

The President was reclining in his seat and had a kind of half-smile on his face, a smile I had often seen when he had to deal with something he would rather not.

"Listen. I hope the Irish people understand the great values of our country. And if they think that a few soldiers represent the entirety of America, they don't really understand America then. There have been great ties between Ireland and America and we've got a lot of Irish Americans here that are very proud of their heritage and their country. But you know, they must not understand if they are angry over Abu Ghraib — if they say this is what America represents, they don't understand our country, because we don't represent that. We are a compassionate country. We're a strong country, and we'll defend ourselves. But we help people. And we've helped the Irish and we'll continue to do so. We've got a good relationship with Ireland."

"And they are angry over Iraq as well and particularly the continuing death toll there," I added, moving him on to the war that had claimed a hundred Iraqi lives that very day. He continued to smile but just barely.

"Well, I can understand that. People don't like war. But what they should be angry about is the fact that there was a brutal dictator there that had destroyed lives and put them in mass graves and torture rooms. Listen, I wish they could have seen the seven men that came to see me in the Oval Office — they had their right hands cut off by Saddam Hussein because the currency had devalued when he was the leader. And guess what happened? An American saw the fact that they had their hands cut off and crosses, or Xs, carved in their forehead. And he flew them to America and they came to my office with a new hand, grateful for the generosity of America, and with Saddam Hussein's brutality in their mind. Look, Saddam Hussein had used weapons of mass destruction against his own people, against the neighbourhood. He was a brutal dictator who posed a threat that the United Nations voted unanimously to say, Mr Saddam Hussein —"

Having noted the tone of my questions, the President had now sat forward in his chair and had become animated, gesturing with his hands for emphasis. But as I listened to the history of Saddam Hussein and the weapons inspectors and the UN resolutions, my heart was sinking. He was resorting to the type of meandering stock answer I had heard scores of times and had hoped to avoid. Going back over this old ground could take two or three minutes and allow him to keep talking without dealing with the current state of the war. It was a filibuster of sorts. With nothing but bad news coming out of Iraq and still no sign of the weapons, I knew that if I didn't challenge him, the interview would be a wasted opportunity.

"But, Mr President, you didn't find any weapons," I interjected.

"Let me finish, let me finish. May I finish?"

With his hand raised, he requested that I stop speaking. He paused and looked me straight in the eye to make sure I had got the message. He wanted to continue, so I backed off and he went on.

"The United Nations said, 'Disarm or face serious consequences'. That's what the United Nations said. And guess what? He didn't disarm. He didn't disclose his arms. And therefore he faced serious consequences. But we have found a capacity for him to make a weapon. See, he had the capacity to make weapons . . ."

I was now beginning to feel shut out of this event. He had the floor and he wasn't letting me dance. My blood was boiling to such a point that I felt like slapping him. But I was dealing with the

President of the United States; and he was too far away anyway. I suppose I had been naïve to think that he was making himself available to me so I could spar with him or plumb the depths of his thought processes. Sitting there, I knew that I was nobody special and that this was just another opportunity for the President to repeat his mantra. He seemed irked to be faced with someone who wasn't nodding gravely at him as he was speaking.

". . . He was dangerous. And no one can argue that the world is better off with Saddam. If Saddam were in power —"

"But Mr President," I interrupted again, "the world is a more dangerous place today. I don't know whether you can see that or not."

"Why do you say that?"

"There are terrorist bombings every single day. It's now a daily event. It wasn't like that two years ago."

"What was it like on September 11th 2001? It was a . . . there was relative calm, we —"

"But it's your response to Iraq that's considered —"

"Let me finish. Let me finish. Please. You ask the questions and I'll answer them, if you don't mind."

His hand was raised again as if to indicate that he was not going to tolerate this. Again, I felt I had no choice but to keep quiet.

"On September 11th 2001, we were attacked in an unprovoked fashion. Everybody thought the world was calm. There have been bombings since then — not because of my response to Iraq. There were bombings in Madrid, there were bombings in Istanbul. There were bombings in Bali. There were killings in Pakistan."

He seemed to be finished, so I took a deep breath and tried once again. So far, facial expressions were defining this interview as much as anything that was said, so I focused on looking as if I was genuinely trying to fathom him.

"Indeed, Mr President, and I think Irish people understand that. But I think there is a feeling that the world has become a more dangerous place because you have taken the focus off

Al Qaeda and diverted into Iraq. Do you not see that the world is a more dangerous place? I saw four of your soldiers lying dead on the television the other day, a picture of four soldiers just lying there without their flak jackets."

"Listen, nobody cares more about death than I do —"

"Is there a point or place —"

"Let me finish. Please. Let me finish, and then you can follow up, if you don't mind." By now he was getting used to the rhythm of this interview and didn't seem quite so taken aback by my attempt to take control of it. "Nobody cares more about death than I do. I care a lot about it. But I do believe the world is a safer place and becoming a safer place. I know that a free Iraq is going to be a necessary part of changing the world." The President seemed to be talking more openly now and from the heart rather than from a script. The history lesson on Saddam Hussein was over. "Listen, people join terrorist organisations because there's no hope and there's no chance to raise their families in a peaceful world where there is not freedom. And so the idea is to promote freedom and at the same time protect our security. And I do believe the world is becoming a better place, absolutely."

I could not tell how much time had elapsed, maybe five or six minutes, so I moved quickly on to the question I most wanted to ask George Bush in person.

"Mr President, you are a man who has a great faith in God. I've heard you say many times that you strive to serve somebody greater than yourself."

"Right."

"Do you believe that the hand of God is guiding you in this war on terror?"

This question had been on my mind ever since September 11th when George Bush began to invoke God in his speeches. He spoke as if he believed that his job of stewarding America through the attacks and beyond was somehow preordained, that he had been chosen for this role. He closed his eyes as he began to answer.

"Listen, I think that God . . . that my relationship with God is a very personal relationship. And I turn to the Good Lord for strength. I turn to the Good Lord for guidance. I turn to the Good Lord for forgiveness. But the God I know is not one that . . . the God I know is one that promotes peace and freedom. But I get great sustenance from my personal relationship." He sat forward again. "That doesn't make me think I'm a better person than you are, by the way. Because one of the great admonitions in the Good Book is, 'Don't try to take a speck out of your eye if I've got a log in my own'."

I suspected that he was also telling me that I should not judge him.

I switched to Ireland again and to the controversy then raging over the Irish government's decision to allow the use of Shannon Airport for the transport of soldiers and weapons to the Gulf.

"You are going to meet Bertie Ahern when you arrive at Shannon Airport tomorrow. I guess he went out on a limb for you, presumably because of the great friendship between our two countries. Can you look him in the eye when you get there and say, 'It will be worth it, it will work out'?"

"Absolutely. I wouldn't be doing this, I wouldn't have made the decision I did if I didn't think the world would be better."

I felt that the President had now become personally involved in this interview, even quoting a Bible passage, so I made one more stab at trying to get inside his head.

"Why is it that others don't understand what you are about?"

He shrugged. "I don't know. History will judge what I'm about."

I could not remember my next question. My mind had gone completely blank. The President had not removed me from his gaze since we had begun and I wanted to keep up the eye contact. If I diverted to my notes on the table beside me, he would know he had flustered me. For what seemed like an eternity, but probably no more than two seconds, I stared at him, searching his eyes for inspiration.

It finally came.

"Can I just turn to the Middle East?"

"Sure."

He talked about his personal commitment to solving that conflict. As he did so, I could see one of the White House crew signalling for me to wrap up the interview, but the President was in full flight.

"Like Iraq, the Palestinian and the Israeli issue is going to require good security measures," he said.

Now out of time, I was fully aware that another question was pushing it, but I would never be here again and I had spent four years covering an administration that appeared to favour Israel at every turn.

"And perhaps a bit more even-handedness from America?" I asked, though it came out more as a comment.

The President did not see the look of horror on the faces of his staff as he began to defend his stance. "I'm the first President to have called for a Palestinian state. That to me sounds like a reasonable and balanced approach. I will not allow terrorists determine the fate, as best I can, of people who want to be free."

Hands were signalling furiously now for me to end the interview.

"Mr President, thank you very much."

"You're welcome," he replied, still half-smiling and half-frowning.

It was over. I felt like a delinquent child who had been reprimanded by a stern, unwavering father. My face must have been the same colour as my suit. Yet I also knew that we had discussed some important issues — probably more candidly than I had heard from President Bush in some time.

I was removing my microphone when he addressed me.

"Is that how you do it in Ireland — interrupting people all the time?"

I froze. He was not happy with me and was letting me know it.

"Yes," I stuttered, determined to maintain my own half-smile.

I was aching to get out of there for a breath of air when I remembered that I had earlier discussed with staff the possibility of having my picture taken with the President. I had been told that, when the interview was over, I could stand up with Mr Bush, and the White House photographer would snap a picture. Not wanting to waste the opportunity, I stood up and asked him to join me.

"Oh, she wants the photograph now," he said from his still-seated position.

He rose, stood beside me and put an arm around my shoulder. Taking his cue, I put an arm up around his shoulder and we both grinned for the cameras.

IN MY HASTE TO LEAVE, I almost forgot the tapes and had to be reminded by the film crew to take them. Outside in the corridor I located Stephanie and the marathon-running intern and we bolted out to the street. Once we cleared the main gate, we ran, high heels and all, across Lafayette Park. Running through rush-hour traffic, I thought that this had to be about as crazy as a journalist's job gets. I had just been admonished by the President of the United States and now I was turning cartwheels in order to get the interview on air. As I dashed past a waste bin, I had a fleeting urge to throw in the tapes and run home instead. My mobile phone rang and I recognised the number as that of my closest friend back in Dublin.

"How did it go?" he asked.

"Terrible," I bawled; "it was horrible." I was panting. He sensed the panic in my voice, but just having him there on the line brought me back to my senses.

At the studio I handed over the tapes and disappeared into the toilet, to take a long, deep breath. I sat there turning it all over in my head and the phone rang again. It was MC, the press officer from the White House, and her voice was cold.

"We just want to say how disappointed we are in the way you conducted the interview," she said.

"How is that?" I asked.

"You talked over the President, not letting him finish his answers."

"Oh, I was just moving him on," I said, explaining that I wanted some new insight from him on the events making world news, not two-year-old answers about Saddam Hussein.

"He did give you plenty of new stuff."

She estimated that I had interrupted the President eight times and added that I had upset him. I was upset too, I told her. The line started to break up; I was in a basement with a bad phone signal. I took her number and agreed to call her back. While the interview was being racked up in another room for live transmission, I dialled the White House number and she was on the line again.

"I'm here with Colby," she indicated.

"Right."

"You were given an opportunity to interview the leader of the free world and you blew it," she began.

I was beginning to feel as if I might be dreaming. "Leader of the free world": the words echoed in my head. I had naïvely believed the American President was referred to as the "leader of the free world" only in an unofficial tongue-in-cheek sort of way by outsiders, and not among his closest staff.

"You were more vicious than any of the White House press corps or even some of them up on Capitol Hill. . . . The President leads the interview," she said.

"I don't agree," I replied, my initial worry now turning to frustration. "It's the journalist's job to lead the interview."

It was suggested that perhaps I could edit the tapes to take out the interruptions, but I made it clear that this would not be possible. As the conversation progressed, I learned that I might find it difficult to secure further co-operation from the White House. A man's voice then came on the line. Colby, I assumed.

"And, it goes without saying, you can forget about the interview with Laura Bush."

I didn't hear what else he said. I was thinking back on his earlier comment about waiting to see how I got on with the President first before deciding to let me loose on Mrs Bush. Clearly the White House had thought they would be dealing with an Irish "colleen" bowled over by the opportunity to interview the Bushes. If anyone there had done their research on RTÉ's interviewing techniques, they might have known better.

MC also indicated that she would be contacting the Irish Embassy in Washington — in other words, an official complaint from Washington to Dublin.

By now the *Prime Time* programme director was trying to get my attention, because the interview was about to air.

"I don't know how we are going to repair this relationship but have a safe trip back to Ireland," MC concluded. I told her I had not meant to upset her since she had been more than helpful to me. The conversation ended.

By the time I got to the control room, the broadcast had just started. It was at the point of the first confrontation with the "leader of the free world" and those gathered around the monitors were glued to it. "Well done," someone said. "This is great."

"YOU FAIRLY RATTLED HIM, so you did," a woman shouted across the arrivals hall at Shannon Airport, when I flew in early the following morning. Well, I thought, somebody was watching. Most of Ireland had been closely following a soccer international between England and Portugal when the interview with the President was aired. Within hours, however, an argument was raging on RTÉ Radio's gabfest, Joe Duffy's *Liveline*. "Rude and unprofessional," complained one guest with an American accent. "Bush was the one who was rude," countered a Dublin listener. "She did us proud." "She blew it." And on it went.

By now the White House had vented its anger to the Irish Embassy in Washington. To make matters worse for the administration, the interview had made its way onto American television. The European Broadcasting Union, an umbrella group of broadcasters, had distributed it as a normal matter of courtesy. CNN was replaying it around the world and by the end of the day it had been aired in Baghdad.

I had got through eighteen years of journalism without generating as much as a single column inch of controversy. As a young reporter training with the *Cork Examiner*, I had been taught to stick to the facts and to be fair. Balanced reporting, I learned, involved airing opposite viewpoints while keeping your own thoughts to yourself. A second school of opinion that was more in vogue in times of war was that any worthwhile journalist should infuse their coverage with something of what they feel in their gut.

I thought about this as I climbed up the steps to RTÉ's live camera position at Dromoland Castle to account for myself on the six o'clock television news. Had I been fair? Was it possible to be neutral in a war situation? Or should I just have been more deferential to George Bush? I felt that I had simply done my job and shuddered at the thought of the backlash I would surely have faced in Ireland had I *not* challenged the President on matters that had changed the way America was viewed around the world.

I watched the comings and goings below in the castle yard. Vans were ferrying people and goods here and there, US secret service agents were blending in with local security, and journalists were loitering in the evening sun. As I turned to leave, I bumped straight into the Taoiseach, Bertie Ahern, who was waiting to go on air.

"Howya," he said, winking.

"I hope this hasn't caused you too much hassle, Taoiseach," I blurted.

Bertie Ahern had steered a steady course supporting Washington's stance on Iraq and had allowed the use of Shannon Airport in the face of bitter opposition and public protests. At an official level at least, he had decided, Ireland would be better served by preserving its historic ties with America.

"Arrah, don't worry at all; you haven't caused me one bit of hassle," Bertie smiled wryly.

I don't know what he said to the President, who reportedly referred to the interview immediately upon arrival, but if Bertie Ahern was annoyed with me or with RTÉ, he didn't show it.

A pesky journalist upsetting the leader of the free world was not the only headache for the American handlers and the Irish government that evening in Dromoland. Tabloid-style photographers were busy in the castle grounds and no sooner had Mr Bush and his wife Laura descended on the stately pile than the President was captured on camera trying to open a stubborn window on the top floor. When he eventually got it to budge, he was clearly visible in his sleeveless white vest, his hair still wet from a shower. Two thousand gardaí and soldiers on patrol could not, it seemed, prevent the media getting a shot of Mr Bush in a state of partial undress in the bedroom. As news of the picture spread around the press pool, the Irish government launched operation "vest wing". RTÉ, which was supervising the international pooled film material, ordered that the picture be recalled. Frantic messages were relayed to other broadcasters warning them against airing the window shot. But anyone diligently recording already had it and some foreign networks had even sent it to air. At the restaurant in the Old Ground Hotel in Ennis, journalists' phones came alive as news of the picture spread, followed immediately by confirmation of RTÉ's decision to ban it. Such a saucy diversion was music to my ears. Perhaps Coleman versus Bush was over?

THE FOLLOWING WEEKEND, HOWEVER, the Irish dailies had all joined the spat over the encounter in the White House Library. "Coleman dishes Bush up a fulsome Irish grill" read one headline. "Bush declares War on RTÉ" said another. RTÉ continued to make international news too, with articles appearing in newspapers from Scotland all the way to Taipei. E-mails and phone calls poured into the offices in Dublin.

> Good Day! Would any recipient of this e-mail kindly inform Ms Coleman that most Americans now consider her completely ignorant and rude and that we really don't give a damn about her liberal views. What we do care about is that she completely embarrassed herself and her country by being such an absolute ass to our President.
>
> Ft Lauderdale, Florida

> I would like to apologise for the rudeness of our moronic President. He is truly an embarrassment. I commend you for the way you conducted your interview.
>
> Pittsburgh, Pennsylvania

> Finally King George gets cornered by a REAL journalist!
>
> Max in Kansas

By the time the leaders' joint press conference rolled around in Dromoland at the end of the EU summit, the sun had come out again, firing up those vivid greens in the Irish landscape which Americans rave about when they tour the Ring of Kerry. The White House press corps was stuck on a bus somewhere en route to the castle from their base in Ennis, delayed by a group of anti-war protestors blocking the road. As we waited for the outdoor event to begin, US administration officials mingled cordially with Irish diplomats. I caught the eye of then Secretary of State Colin Powell. He was grinning at me. A White House official who had conducted a briefing in the West Wing days earlier raised his brow as he passed by but said nothing. First Lady Laura Bush arrived, nodding to everyone, followed by a dutifully sombre-looking Condoleezza Rice. I took a seat with the press pack just in front of the podium where Mr Bush and Mr Ahern were due to speak.

Now dried off and fully dressed, the President appeared a lot more relaxed than when I had last seen him. But in stark contrast to the reception given to previous American presidents like Ronald Reagan and John F. Kennedy, Ireland wasn't proving to be an easy place for Mr Bush. President Mary McAleese had made it clear that she was concerned about the treatment of prisoners in Iraq and Bertie Ahern publicly raised the subject of the detainees at Guantanamo Bay. However, not wishing to outshine his guest in the elocution stakes, he mangled the pronunciation, leaving everyone wondering where the hell "Guantapanama" was! Beside me in the press section, *Irish Independent* writer Miriam Lord fidgeted as she wracked her brains for a line of colour material for her column.

"I dare ya ask Bush a question," she whispered in my ear.

"Would ya feck off, Miriam!"

"Ah go on. Just to see how he reacts."

I didn't take the bait. My fifteen minutes of notoriety had already lasted longer than I had anticipated or wanted.

THE PRESIDENTIAL ENTOURAGE sped off from Dromoland in a blaze of flashing lights and screaming sirens and I returned to my little world on the street called M in Washington. To avoid any confusion in the nation's capital, or perhaps to create it, streets are named after the letters of the alphabet.

I felt a tad more conspicuous than when I'd left for Ireland. I was quickly alerted to the fact that the popular internet search engine Google had returned over one hundred thousand results for the subject of the interview! In cyberspace, the twelve-minute encounter with the President took on a life of its own as bloggers ranted and raved. The vast majority of these internet commentators felt it was time a reporter had challenged Mr Bush.

Back at the White House, the fact that I had been asked to submit questions prior to the interview generated enquiries from the American press corps. "Any time a reporter sits down with the

President they are welcome to ask him whatever questions they want to ask," White House Press Secretary Scott McClellan told CBS correspondent Bill Plante.

"Yes, but that's beside the point," replied Plante.

Under repeated questioning, McClellan conceded that other staff members might have asked for questions. "Certainly there will be staff-level discussion, talking about what issues reporters may want to bring up in some of these interviews. I mean that happens all the time."

I had not been prevented from asking any of my questions. The only topics I had been warned away from were the Bush daughters Jenna and Barbara, regular fodder for the tabloids at the time, and Michael Moore — none of which was on my list. Moore's documentary *Fahrenheit 9/11*, which was playing in American cinemas, was the last thing the Bush administration needed in the run-up to the 2004 election. It alleged a close relationship between the Bushes and the Saudi royal family, bearing in mind that most of the September 11th hijackers were Saudis. The film asked why the Bin Laden family had been flown out of the US days after the attacks and it lambasted politicians for not sending their own sons to Iraq. Moore had noticed RTÉ's interview with the President and in the weeks that followed urged American journalists to follow the example of "that Irish woman". A full ten days after the interview, President Bush and I, though probably never likely to meet face-to-face again, were still making news together. *The New York Times* (4 July 2004) devoted an editorial to the interview under the headline "When Irish eyes stop smiling":

> The planners of President Bush's recent European summit trip may have envisioned a pleasant inning of softball questions when they pencilled in a brief interview with RTÉ, the state television of Ireland, first stop on his tour. What they got was the intrepid Carole Coleman, RTÉ's Washington correspondent, firing follow-up questions about death and destruction in Iraq. . . . The White House later protested to the Irish Embassy, but her

employers gave Ms Coleman a well-done, and so do we. The colloquy, as the Irish say, was a sight for sore eyes — an American President who seldom holds a White House news conference unexpectedly subjected to some muscular European perspective.

In a way, Irish eyes had stopped smiling for President Bush, as had many other sets of eyes around the world and at home.

But at that stage most Americans still saw things differently. They had lost two thousand seven hundred people on September 11th and regarded their President as a good man battling against evil. As for Saddam Hussein, it didn't matter that he had not attacked New York and Washington. It was enough that he was the type who might.

Over the coming year I would find that in supporting the President and ultimately re-electing him, Americans chiefly wanted to believe in themselves. They didn't want to hear that American policy was inciting extremists. They wanted the idealism that George Bush provided. More than anything else, they desperately wanted to hold on to their belief that they were still part of the greatest country on earth, God's country.

Chapter 2

Leaving DC

"*T*hat handbag is too big, Ma'am. Did you not see the specifications on the sign?"

The policewoman at the security check on Pennsylvania Avenue was pointing to the outline of a rectangle indicating the official specifications for handbags. Well, I had seen it, but not until I had got there. What did she want me to do, shrink the bag? I decided to keep the thought to myself.

"I'm sorry," I said, putting on my really-I-didn't-know-ma'am face. She summoned a colleague for a consultation. "Let her through. Just check the contents," he said. With a white surgical glove on one hand and a stick in the other, she poked through my makeup, notebook, pens and assorted bits and pieces and finally drew something out. I swallowed hard.

"What's this?" she asked, holding up a small black cylinder.

"It's a device to prevent you, eh, I mean me, from getting attacked," I stuttered. She examined it and waited for me to say something further.

"It makes a loud noise," I added, trying to be helpful.

Immediately I knew I had said the wrong thing. "Attack" and "loud noise" were not sounding very smart, not today of all days. The item in question was a device about four inches long, which when pressed at both ends emitted a shrill scream. It was designed to attract attention, if you were approached by a hostile stranger in the street at night. I had just put it in my bag the previous week. Bad move.

"Is it an aerosol?" She was snarling now.

"I don't think so."

My friend Mary from Cork was anxiously looking back from the far side of the security fence. The policewoman shot me an icy glance and announced that she was confiscating the black cylinder. Thankful that I had not been wrestled to the ground and hand-cuffed, I nodded and walked out through the fence to wait for the arrival of the President of the United States. It was a freezing January day and George W. Bush was being sworn in for a second term.

I had witnessed his first inauguration from the top of a rain-soaked media platform — the safest place to be, given the hordes of angry protestors who did not accept him as the legitimately elected President. The disputed result of the 2000 election and the eventual Supreme Court decision to award Florida's vote (and consequently the Presidency) to the Republican candidate had angered the fifty per cent of Americans who had voted for Al Gore. This time around, despite now being inextricably associated with Mr Bush as a result of the interview, I went as a member of the public with no special access. After all, ordinary people drag their kids from the far side of the country every four years to witness this exercise in democracy. The least I could do was walk down from Dupont Circle.

My friend and I found a spot along Pennsylvania Avenue, where the President was due to pass after his swearing-in ceremony on Capitol Hill. A double row of metal barriers separated us from the parade route, but they were low enough for us to see over. That was to change. No sooner had we arrived than groups of highway patrolmen, police officers and marines started to appear — first in batches of ten, then twenty and thirty — to take up position behind the barriers. Now we were staring directly into the faces of cops standing shoulder to shoulder barely three feet in front of us. By the time they had all assembled, there was a wall of law enforcement along the entire length of America's main street. We would have to watch the inaugural parade through the gaps between their necks.

But this was freedom — or so President Bush suggested that cold January day — freedom to make the journey to the event that is the crowning glory of a democracy, only to be blocked from seeing anything by armed uniformed men. For several days beforehand, jet fighters had patrolled the skies over the capital and anti-aircraft technology had been placed at secret locations around its perimeter. There were as many security guards as visitors in town. Washington was like a city under siege.

Since his first inauguration in January 2001, deep divisions had remained over George Bush's presidency and policies. After the terrorist attacks of September 11th 2001, America had united firmly behind him, seeing leadership qualities that surprised even his detractors. But the country had split again over the decision to invade Iraq without the sanction of the United Nations or a proper post-war plan. By the time the 2004 election rolled around, US forces in Iraq were bogged down in a bloody insurgency, but most Americans wanted only the positive spin. And that's what the President gave them.

"The survival of liberty in our land depends on the success of liberty in other lands," he declared in his inaugural address. Buoyed by movements towards freedom in Lebanon and Ukraine, Mr Bush went even further, saying he was putting all brutal regimes on notice. The suggestion was that the days when America did business with dictators, and when the CIA supported (and even created) them, were over. America would show it was the good guy.

"All who live in tyranny and hopelessness can know the United States will not ignore your oppression or excuse your oppressors." The crowd politely applauded. During his first four years in office, the country had become even more polarised culturally and geographically, with people in the South and Midwest distancing themselves from the values and lifestyles of those they branded as the liberal elites on the coasts. America had become two nations, red versus blue. George Bush and John Kerry epitomised the divide. Bush with his simple message — family and country first — and Kerry with his convoluted and at times contradictory shades of grey. Bush told voters that America was still righteous and strong, and destined to do great things in the world. John Kerry told them that the United States was on the wrong track, was drowning in debt and had lost respect abroad. Fifty-four million Americans believed the bad news and cast their votes accordingly. But fifty-nine million distrusted Kerry, concluding that he and his haughty, over-educated band of followers were not on America's side at all. They chose the doctor who gave them the best diagnosis. That was all before the lack of a proper plan to bring peace to Iraq was fully brought home to Americans and before the racial poverty and general ineptitude exposed by Hurricane Katrina made the patient look rather sickly.

Then there were the issues of character and faith, and George Bush had taken ownership of these from the start. When he rolled up his sleeves, he looked like a man of the people. When John Kerry did the same, it seemed contrived. George Bush had carved out an image as a tough yet God-fearing man; someone who knew deep inside that his was not the ultimate authority. John Kerry preferred to keep the higher powers out of politics. Though Republican voters do attend church more regularly than do Democrats, many of them lump all Democrats into the "heathen on a fast track to hell" category. Yet four out of every five Americans believe in God, the highest percentage in the western world. What they disagree over is His place in public life. God was mentioned three times in the President's inaugural speech, with further references to the Maker of Heaven and Earth and the Sermon on the Mount. It was at such times that the huge gulf between America and Europe on matters of faith was most apparent.

To many Americans listening on that day, George Bush was still a misguided megalomaniac. His talk of spreading democracy like honey was seen as rhetoric to shore up the latest rationale for the bloodshed in Iraq. While Saddam Hussein had been dragged ignominiously out of a rat hole and had had his hair examined for lice before the entire world, Americans and Iraqis were still dying in a conflict about which many remained deeply sceptical. The administration, they felt, would never have gone to this trouble to rescue a poor African country that wasn't sitting on top of oil reserves. Furthermore, bringing God into the equation set off alarm bells that America, whether intentionally or not, was sending a message to Muslims that this was a religious war.

But to the converted, the President's words were like those of a political messiah sent to them from Texas with the moral clarity of the saints and the prophets. They were the words of one who, like Jesus himself, had endured condemnation but would come to be judged by history as a man of courage and conviction. Far from worrying the faithful, the frequent references to the Almighty calmed and reassured them.

Though defining the world's view of George Bush's America, the war in Iraq was not the main concern among those who re-elected him. And no wonder. The vast majority of Americans have remained largely unaffected by the conflict. Those fighting the war and their immediate relatives account for just a tiny percentage of the US population. The involvement of the majority is restricted to ideologically supporting or opposing the war or digesting the latest death toll figures coming out of Iraq. Unprecedented government controls and a tamed media have joined forces to ensure that the unpleasant side of the war is kept hidden. For many, faith has been more important than war and the issue of values at home is as urgent as anything the US is doing abroad. America's current obsession is God.

"THE PRESIDENT IS COMING INTO VIEW," a voice bellowed over a loudspeaker. By now, we were so cold that our breath was freezing as it hit the air, and we could no longer feel our feet. As we lined up cameras, craning between the necks of the police for a clear view, there was a sudden flurry of activity. Security men and secret service agents, walking ahead of the presidential motorcade, began to run. As they passed us, they were jogging, in their long trench coats with the black limousines gliding silently behind them. There was some hesitant cheering from spectators who wondered what was going on. It turned out that some vocal opposition to Mr Bush a few blocks back had caused the motorcade to abruptly speed up and drive on. He had passed us and was gone. We saw nothing, not even the briefest wave from a bullet-proof window. All the Commander-in-Chief could have seen were the backsides of the police officers standing to attention along the avenue.

I had not quite managed to figure out George W. Bush. One day I thought I understood his view of the world; the next I was hopelessly lost again. Just when I would allow myself to think that he might be a genuine visionary, he would do or say something that got me wondering again about his competence and his real motives. Oil, faith, power? I decided on that freezing January day to use some time off from my television work to travel to those parts of America where President Bush is regarded more as messiah than misguided megalomaniac and where faith is even more important than politics.

As a vaguely compliant Catholic, from a country where to talk openly of a personal relationship with God means that you are somehow suspect, I wanted to visit places where to be called a religious fundamentalist is a badge of honour. I wanted to see "red America", where everything is actually in black and white, and to meet Americans who had never been to New York and had no desire to go there, believing it to represent all that is wrong with western society. I also wanted to see the America where Muslims, Jews and Christians could live together despite their differences. I planned to visit groups like the Mormons and the Amish who value their freedom to live as they choose, and who believe George Bush is the best person to preserve that freedom. Most of all, I wanted to touch down in the sort of out-of-the-way towns that planes usually fly over on their way to somewhere else. For four years I had travelled throughout the States, but still I felt as though I had been living inside the Washington bubble. It was time to leave the city.

IT WAS BREAKFAST TIME in America, my favourite time of day to eat out. I was having corned beef hash, topped with two eggs, over-easy, and little triangles of wheat toast — no butter, thanks. Without invitation, the waiter refilled my mug with steaming hot coffee. Here, they assume you will drink at least three cups.

"OK customers, listen up." A man dressed in a white shirt, black waistcoat, bowtie and flat green cap grabbed a microphone from behind the counter. "This won't take long, and I guarantee you it will get your day off to a good start. Everybody now please stand." Knowing the drill, the regulars scrambled quickly to their feet, hands on hearts. The out-of-towners like me were still consulting one another with puzzled looks as what proved to be a daily ritual proceeded.

"I pledge allegiance to the flag of the United States of America, and to the republic for which it stands, one nation under God, indivisible, with liberty and justice for all. Thank you, and have a good day." A loud cheer went up around the diner and everybody went back to their eggs.

"Hi, I'm an Irish writer," I said, introducing myself to the man with the microphone.

"Hi, I'm a Jewish deli owner," he shot back.

That's how I met Ted Levitt, owner of Chick 'n' Ruth's Deli, an institution in the Maryland town of Annapolis. Every morning for fifteen years, he has been asking his customers to recite the pledge of allegiance with him. Ted is an elf-like man with glasses who likes to talk the ear off everyone who comes in the door. "I wanted to do something I thought was right," he said, echoing a sentiment I had heard so many times since moving to America for the second time in January 2001. In the late 1980s I had spent two years working in radio in Massachusetts, but had encountered nothing like the sense of moral responsibility now gripping the country. Since September 11th, in particular, doing the right thing or standing up for a long-held value, no matter what the consequences, is now regarded as a solemn duty by many Americans. Ted had decided to take a stand when he discovered that his son's school had dropped the daily recitation of the pledge following the objection of two other parents. "So they had to drop it for everybody," he said, recalling the rage he had felt that a tiny minority was now dictating whether or not the majority could honour their country and their God. Ted joined me in the corner booth and talked as I finished my breakfast.

"What if I come to your church, and I'm Jewish? I'll still sit down out of respect when you do. I might not say your prayer, but I'll stand when you stand, kneel when you kneel. Now everyone is so focused on what's politically correct. When somebody does something wrong, everybody kicks up a fuss; when you do something right, nobody pays any attention to it."

Any mention of God these days and some Americans are upset. They feel this elevates Christianity over other faiths and that God should have no public place in a country whose citizens practise everything from traditional faiths to witchcraft.

Ted Levitt, who dishes up pastrami on rye to Jews and gentiles alike, was shaking his head in frustration. "Your God is whomever you believe in. I'll ask people what they believe in. If they say nothing, that's fine. Then 'nothing' is their God. I believe religion was invented to bring people together. Whether you are going to the synagogue or praying to a statue of Buddha at home with your family, you are doing something together."

Chick 'n' Ruth's is an old-fashioned establishment and a magnet for local politicians. Every Maryland Governor since the 1960s has dined there and left their autographed photo on the wall as proof. As we chatted, a former Mayor of Annapolis came over to shake Ted's hand.

"Mayor Hopkins," said Ted, saluting the elderly man. I had seen a plaque dedicated to Hopkins downtown and assumed that he was dead, but here the more things you can stick your name on before you pass on, the better.

"And who is this?" asked the Mayor, taking my hand.

"This is my girl. Find your own girl."

Mayor Hopkins shuffled away laughing. "He's Al Hopkins but I call him Mayor," said Ted, explaining that he prefers to use titles and last names as a way of showing respect. Ted learned courtesy and business from his parents Chick and Ruth Levitt who had started the deli forty years earlier. Ted was just eight years old then but reckons he has worked there every single day since the doors opened. Just talking to him, you can tell he is a bit obsessive. Work is his play and he has no time for wasters. As well as putting in ninety hours a week at the deli, he runs a pretzel factory on the side and restores old cars at night. "I don't watch television," he volunteered by way of explanation. Ted was certain that the loss of hard work was dragging America down — he could even see it in the deli, where getting good staff was becoming more difficult. A one-eyed waitress wearing a black patch and a four-foot-tall waiter whose sparkling personality made up for his lack of height were among Ted's most loyal workers, remaining in the business while others came and went.

"I don't think America can stay being the country it was built to be and has the reputation of being," he reflected, throwing an eye up to the portrait of his father on the wall. Chick Levitt doesn't look to be quite the character his son is, and you get the feeling he'd be proud to see the long lines of customers outside his old place. "I know he doesn't like it when I have to yell at the employees," said Ted pensively as though remembering a time when everybody jumped to attention whenever the boss appeared.

It's not easy to get Ted Levitt to stop talking once he gets going. He's like one of those cab drivers who wants you to know what he thinks and why. Ted prefers tradition to modernity. He values respect and elbow grease. He loves his country but fears the loss of the American dream. Eventually he got called away to resolve a problem at the cash register.

"See you again, sir," I said as he dashed off.

"That's OK. You can call me Ted," he shouted back.

ANNAPOLIS IS SITUATED on the Chesapeake Bay, about an hour's drive east of Washington DC. It has a rich political and military history, being home to the nation's oldest working statehouse and the US Naval Academy, where Navy and Marine officers are trained. For a brief period, from 1783 to 1784, it was the American capital and still has the look of a place where things of great importance occurred. The Treaty of Paris was signed here in 1783, ending the American War of Independence between the thirteen British colonies and the Kingdom of Great Britain. General George Washington also resigned his commission as Commander-in-Chief of the Continental Army in Annapolis before going on to become President of the United States. The town's immaculately maintained colonial homes and gardens speak of an era when America was young and excited about its fledgling democracy. More excited perhaps than it is now.

"Ladies and gentlemen, please stand for the Honourable Robert Ehrlich." Over two hundred and twenty years later, the Republican Governor of Maryland strode into the very same chamber to deliver his annual State of the State address. Having elected Democrats to Maryland's highest office for the previous four decades, voters had now elevated a Republican, reflecting the party's successes in Washington and around the country. Maryland is still part of blue or Democratic America, but is turning red around the edges.

Ehrlich has the look of a dashing young senator, the type Robert Redford might have played in a movie in his younger days. It was clear by the chatter still continuing in the chamber that his audience was expecting the usual recitation of his achievements, along with the perennial disclaimer about the sorry condition of the state's finances. But Ehrlich must have had the hash and eggs at Chick 'n' Ruth's for breakfast, because he had ditched the agenda and hijacked Ted Levitt's favourite topic — respect. Eye-balling his fellow lawmakers, the Governor launched into an angry diatribe about the lack of respect in politics today and in particular the lack of respect for him. Turns out that, because he was a Republican and most of the senators and congressmen were not, he couldn't get very much of the people's business done. "Capitol Hill, assassin-type politics has no place in the state legislature. It is damaging all of us," he said, scouring the chamber with his eyes. The uncooperative Democrats on the receiving end of this offen-sive were mainly middle-aged men and women, both black and white. A female senator, a mature-looking blonde, sat cross-legged in the front row showing off plenty of ultra-sheer stocking, while throughout the speech a bald congressman chewed gum so fiercely that every muscle in his face and head was given a full workout.

I was surprised to be hearing the same sniping I had become accustomed to in Washington. It was well known that the fit of to-getherness brought on by September 11th had disappeared soon after. But since President Bush's re-election, relations between the two parties had become openly hostile, with each side trying to block the other at every turn. Clearly, at local level, things were no different. As the Governor left the chamber to muted applause, Republicans lauded his outburst as courageous, while Democrats knocked one another down to get to the waiting cameras and de-nounce it as the worst speech they had ever heard. It was clear that any hope of respect breaking out in the Maryland statehouse had already floated out the door into the frigid January air.

OUT THERE THE REAL STATE OF THE STATE was on show. Shivering in the snow and ice, hundreds of people of all ages and races were loudly demanding that lawmakers introduce an amendment to ban gay marriage in the state. Though Democratic, Maryland has an expanding base of conservative Christians who are working overtime to have their voices heard.

"Shake hands with your neighbour," a voice blared across the public address system. I shook hands with a schoolteacher in a fedora who had skipped class to bring his two young sons to the protest.

"It's not that I've anything against gays," he said, "I work with three or four of them and I respect them. I just don't want them forcing their beliefs on me. I'm here for my kids and my country." He was more worried about the war at home than the one abroad — believing his values were as much under attack from gays as from terrorists. Gail Fielder, a woman of about sixty, was buttoned up to her chin in ski gear, but she still looked frozen. "I work with children and I want them protected," she said, regarding me suspiciously when I asked what insanity had brought her from the far end of the state on the most bitterly cold day of the year.

The debate over same-sex marriage burst into the public arena in 2004 when the Supreme Court in Massachusetts ruled that gay couples should be allowed to marry. This led to similar rulings in California and Oregon, where lesbian and gay couples rushed to tie the knot. Many of those marriages were subsequently nullified as frantic battles moved back and forth between the courts and the local governments. Family values groups were fuming that marriage was being "stolen" by gays. President Bush tried introducing a constitutional amendment to define marriage as a union between a man and a woman only. It didn't go anywhere in his first term, but became a major issue with conservative voters — maybe the most significant issue — in the 2004 presidential race. On election day, ten states, perhaps in a ploy to get conservative voters to the polls, held referenda on banning gay marriage. In all ten, including Georgia, Michigan, Oklahoma, Ohio and Oregon, the people voted for the ban.

THE SNOW HAD BEEN PELTING DOWN even more heavily in the town of Arlington, Vermont, one year earlier when I had witnessed the civil union of two middle-aged women after ten years together as a couple. A civil union, offered in the liberal state of Vermont in the north-east, is a step below marriage, giving gay couples enhanced rights, but not something they can actually call a marriage. The union is recognised in Vermont but not in any other state. All day, as a foot of fresh snow transformed Arlington into a postcard scene, Cindy and Amy arranged seats and music and hairdos for their evening ceremony at a quaint Victorian inn. Amy, a stout woman with a mane of shaggy auburn hair, was the elder partner. She was a mother of two children, and grandmother to fourteen-month-old Conor, who toddled off laughing hysterically whenever anyone went near him. Both women had diamond engagement rings but Amy wore the trousers and Cindy, a short blonde, got to wear the white dress.

"We are as committed to one another as any couple, yet we feel we are discriminated against," Amy said, as the couple readied themselves in an upstairs room. Even though they would be returning to New York, where their union was illegal, the following day, they wanted to go through with the ceremony just to make their point. "Look at Britney Spears," exclaimed Cindy, suddenly getting teary. "She has a right to marry. And her marriage can last just forty-eight hours and that's OK. But we, who are a loving couple committed to one another for a very long time, have no such right."

"She is the love of my life," said Amy, taking her bride's hand in hers to calm her. "I hope she'll spend the next fifty years with me."

"What about God and the Bible?" I asked, wondering if they thought it possible to be both God-fearing and gay. "I do believe in God," said Amy, "but I believe certain people are born the way they are for a reason and I believe I was born this way and shouldn't have fewer rights than others if I choose to be married to Cindy." By now the younger bride-to-be had arranged her blonde curls in a diamond tiara. "The Bible was written at a certain time in history, but things have changed," Cindy added.

Over their ten years together, the two women felt that Americans had become more tolerant. At first Cindy's own mother had not accepted the situation. Eventually she came around and would shortly be giving her daughter away at the ceremony. But while some people had got used to the idea that gays should have equal rights, others opposed it. Both Cindy and Amy were certain that any chance of full gay marriage becoming legal in the US was still decades away.

That evening the two women came downstairs, Amy in a black tuxedo and Cindy in her traditional wedding dress. Before a justice of the peace, they exchanged rings, shed tears and vowed to have and to hold for as long as both should live. "It's about love, having someone to grow old with on the porch," enthused Amy as they took the floor, before forty guests, for their first dance.

LOUIS SHELDON'S EYEBALLS WERE POPPING out of his head at the notion that love or growing old together had anything to do with it. Sitting in his office close to Capitol Hill, the seventy-year-old founder of the Traditional Values Coalition explained it from his viewpoint.

"To begin with the body parts don't fit." He jammed his fingers together to demonstrate. "Look. It's very clear that God intended man and woman to unite in marriage to procreate." Sheldon blamed the growing crisis on judges who, he believed, had allowed homosexuals to think they were a minority suffering discrimination. "There is nothing immutable about the way you have sex," he bellowed, his face turning a bright shade of red. "It's not like the colour of skin or eye formation or other racial characteristics. It's a dysfunctional behaviour." Sheldon mimicked gays and lesbians begging for acceptance. "Please accept me, please don't condemn me." He wasn't going to condemn them, he claimed, "but if they steal marriage from us, they will see how upset we will get".

Sheldon, though extreme in his views, is on the same side as the majority in America. Two-thirds of Americans believe gays should not be allowed to marry. Before coming to the United States, I had always assumed that the US was the market leader when it came to pushing out such boundaries. That was the impression created by the media and Hollywood — in America you can do anything you want. Now the country is to the forefront in holding the line. While Canada and Spain have just legalised gay marriage, the US seems to be going in the opposite direction. For many Americans, turning the clock back is the new definition of progress.

OUTSIDE THE STATEHOUSE A BLACK PASTOR took over the microphone and warmed up the frozen crowd. "We are in a moral war," he roared.

"That's right!" the crowd yelled back.

"The great state of Maryland will define what happens next in this debate," he continued, to chants of "Alleluia Alleluia" from a group of African Americans who were now joining hands and starting to pray in a circle.

"The cross was lifted up and blood was shed, so our lives would be set free from every sin," the pastor declared.

"That's right, that's right!" The crowd was rapturous.

The woman in the ski gear was back beside me with a blanket and two friends.

"You from Ireland?" asked one of them.

"Yes."

"We are from the Radical Sheep Ministry and we have been praying for your country." From the pocket of her coat the woman produced a business card for the Radical Sheep, a prayer group in Baltimore. She normally carried around stones from Ireland to help her pray, but she didn't have them on her today.

"I'll look you up on the web," I said and made to leave.

"One minute. Could you lay your hands on me, so I can continue to pray for Ireland?" she asked. I laughed, bemused by the request, but it looked like she wasn't leaving without being anointed. Checking that there were no cameras around to record my inaugural laying of hands, I removed a glove, placed my palm on her shoulder and with my head bowed I waited for some help from the Radical Sheep. There was silence. I didn't know what to say and no one uttered a word, they just stood there, all of them with their eyes closed, waiting.

Finally I delivered my blessing. "That you may continue to pray for Ireland," I mumbled.

"Thank you, thank you," the woman said and they all disappeared back into the crowd.

I was only an hour from Washington, but already I could tell I was in another world.

Chapter 3

Mansions Await

A billboard message greets travellers to the town of Monroe, Georgia. In large black letters it reads: "A dusty Bible leads to dirty lives."

Ouch! That hurt.

In secondary school I had a Bible. I memorised bits of it as required and then forgot them again. There was no exam in religious knowledge then, so it could not have been important. When I finished school, I packed the Bible away somewhere with the rest of my school texts. I don't remember where. I would wager that by now it is pretty dusty.

"Worship Saturday 5.30. All welcome," continues the "dusty Bible" sign. "Seek and you shall find" urges another sign a hundred yards up the road, indicating that redemption is just around the next corner, if only you can see the evil of your ways and beg forgiveness. The sentiments are nothing if not direct. You get the feeling that they don't get many lukewarm enquiries about the business of deliverance here. You are either getting saved in Monroe, Georgia, or you are not. Before I would leave the town, I would be repeatedly challenged and nudged by these slogans from on high, messages delivered down by middlemen whose business is spreading the word and filling pews. In fact, in the church I had come to visit I would find a maxim that could have been meant only for me. From the wall of the restroom I would be warned that "Christianity is a pilgrimage — not a sightseeing tour".

There's not much sightseeing here. Monroe is a nice little town with a couple of restored plantation houses tucked away on leafy side streets. Like most American towns big or small, it has been turned inside out. What used to be in the centre has fled to the suburbs and vice versa. Essential shopping has moved out to the malls while the pawnbrokers, antique dealers and tattoo parlours, which used to languish at the town limits, have come in to take their place. The two hardware stores that still maintain a custom on the main street seem to specialise in wooden rocking chairs and confederate flags. There's one modern café where the well-heeled half of the town are having lunch and lattes, and a "family restaurant" which does a decent evening trade with the meat-and-potatoes crowd. There are no pubs or sports bars and no evidence of alcohol for sale anywhere. Up at the north end of town, Monroe's black population, fifty per cent, subsists in dreary ramshackle roadside homes, as far away from prosperity as one could get. The only two African Americans I spotted downtown were marked men — dressed in orange jackets and black-and-white striped pants, they were sunning themselves on a bench outside the judicial centre, any ambition to abscond from detention having deserted them long ago.

I was there on a religious sightseeing tour of sorts. I was meeting Stephen Butler, with whom I had come in contact through a website on youth gospel singing. At twenty-three years old, he is an accomplished musician, and a trainee pastor — which in the Baptist tradition is a full-time job — and a self-proclaimed member of the Christian right. That weekend he was hosting a gospel-singing convention at his father's church. Not the "raise the roof" and "praise the Lord" gospel familiar to America's inner cities — this is white evangelical worship, where more and more Americans are finding their spiritual home.

Evangelicals are among those Christians who believe that the Bible is the literal word of God. They argue that there is no need for the filtered interpretation of theologians or church authorities. It means exactly what it says, written in black and white. This rigid adherence to the Word pits them against more mainstream Christians who think the Bible should be read critically. Evangelicals or Christian conservatives do not wonder about the way things are; they rely on certainties. Put simply, they believe that if they accept Jesus as their personal saviour, He will return one day and take them to heaven, as foretold in the Book of Revelations. On the other hand, anyone who does not accept Him will be left behind.

Depending on who you listen to, between thirty and sixty million Americans out of the total population of almost three hundred million are fully fledged evangelicals. These are mainly white, nearly all Protestant and, though spread across the fifty states, most reside in the South and in the heartland. Evangelicals argue that theirs is a simple Christian worldview. Human life is a gift from God which cannot be tampered with. Abortion and stem cell research are wrong, although the death penalty is justified. They feel that God intended marriage as a union between a man and a woman only and that homosexual relations are an abomination. They back the individual's freedom, and in the case of Iraq, America's duty to bring that freedom to others. But most of all, evangelical Christians believe in heaven. Their main goal is to get there.

Because of their entry into politics and public life, evangelicals are a rising power. Far from being private practitioners of their faith, they believe they have a God-given duty to spread the word and save others from an apocalyptic fate. When they turn on their televisions, they see a spiritual battle raging all around, a culture war which, if not fought, will see them destroyed. In their eyes

America's Christians are being persecuted and their values being knocked down by secular forces seeking to dominate Washington and public life.

Stephen's church is located at the back-end of Monroe. To get there, I had to pass a huge grain elevator straddling a rail track, once a bustling commercial centre, but now rusty and idle. I followed a road where wooden houses in danger of being swallowed by weeds stand next to sturdy brick homes with perfectly manicured gardens. So often on the outer edges of town, American neighbourhoods are a mixed bag of decadence and decay — part Wisteria Lane, part Skid Row. With early March bringing the first hint of watery sun, the swinging chairs popular in the south were reappearing on front porches. I passed an art deco gas station, standing proudly like the sort of relic that might still survive along old Route 66 but was pumping nothing here, and then finally I spotted the familiar white spire of a Baptist church. I was way off the beaten track, but this was where the action was that night.

I pulled into the almost empty parking lot and was surprised to find that the church inside was a hive of activity. Food, a focus of most church events in America, was being brought in by a back door, name tags and hymn books were being prepared for visitors from neighbouring Alabama, Tennessee and Florida, and T-shirts with more Christian messages were on display. These slogans were even more direct: "Friends don't let friends go to hell"; "Arrest me, I prayed at school today".

I located Stephen Butler in the hallway, overseeing three different tasks at once. He is baby-faced, yet stands tall and well-built and exudes a quiet air of leadership. He was dressed in a smart tan suit with his short hair gelled into spikes. His father has been the pastor and manager here for three decades and some day Stephen will take over from him.

He led me proudly into the chapel. "Tell me about gospel singing," I whispered, but Stephen waved a hand to indicate that there was no need for such reverence here. Gospel music had intrigued me, because in many states its popularity has spread out far beyond the church doors. Gospel is being played on Christian radio and is moving up the charts. Christian rock music has cornered a large part of the music market, turning church-trained choir boys into stars. In the Deep South, barbershop quartets are as popular with evangelical youth as rap artists are in the cities.

Giving me a brief history lesson, Stephen explained that gospel began as an art form in the seventeenth and eighteenth centuries when people sang from "shape notes". Unlike the round notes most people learn in piano class, the written notes of gospel music are still shaped like triangles, diamonds and semicircles. But the big attraction is the subject matter. Gospel has plenty of love lyrics — but we're talking God's love here.

"The songs are centred on Jesus Christ and the message of the Bible. They tell of death on the cross, the resurrection and the hope we all have for heaven. Some of the songs are upbeat and some so sad they can make you cry," Stephen elaborated in his southern accent.

As we talked, he kept an ear on the soundchecks going on at the microphones while filling me in on his family background. In the 1940s his grandfather Talmadge Butler sang in a gospel quartet and they needed a pianist. A local girl named June obliged and they subsequently married. "At the time there were schools to teach the music and songs of the gospel tradition, but they faded out. Then in the 1990s they started to make a comeback, so my grandmother sent me to one over in Nashville, Tennessee, to study piano and singing."

For Stephen tradition and religion is the family business. He grew up in this church and claimed he had been "saved" there while still a very young child.

"When I was five years old I accepted Jesus Christ as my saviour and from that time everything pointed me in the direction to serve in a ministry," he told me. I didn't know children needed to be saved or born again, but here in Georgia it's not unusual.

"Yes. It happens at a different age for different people. You have to realise you are a sinner. . . . God's word tells us that the penalty for sin is death, and death is hell, so there is no way out but through Jesus Christ. Some people see it at a young age. Others never do. At five years old I heard this and I realised I didn't have a way to heaven except through Christ. So I accepted him as my saviour. That is, 'born again', saved — same thing."

The idea of being born again is not new. It dates back to the Bible itself. In John 3:3, Jesus mentions the idea to Nicodemus, who is startled and wonders if Jesus is asking him to get back into his mother's womb. But Jesus explains that he is talking about entering into a relationship with God, through faith. Virtually all Americans who say they are evangelical claim to have been saved. Millions who are not evangelical or part of the Christian right also claim to be "born again" or to have experienced a spiritual conversion. "Except a man be born again he cannot see the Kingdom of God." This one line from the Bible convinces evangelicals that no matter how much money a man gives to charity or what good works he does, if he doesn't accept Christ as his personal saviour, he has no hope of making it to the next life. President Bush claims to have been born again in his early forties.

Stephen Butler is well aware that much of the western world and many fellow Americans regard him and the evangelical movement with suspicion and even ridicule, but this does not bother him. "Sure, many consider us fundamentalist, but it only means that you live by God's word. People would probably consider me a crazy, but Christ changed my life."

Temptation seems to have turned its back on Stephen. He has never drunk a beer or smoked a cigarette and told me he never wanted to, even as a teenager when most people rebel and experiment. "Being saved at a young age kept me from a lot of things. God's word purifies me and points out what's wrong in my life, so when things are clearly wrong, I stay away from them," he said, making it all sound very easy. Having avoided all youthful distractions, twenty-three-year-old Stephen is already married and on his way to becoming a family man and a respected spiritual leader. "Me and my wife have had some tough times, but we have prayed and accepted Christ, and know he will look after us." This confidence, he added, comes from reading the Bible. "I read it every day . . . read all sixty-six books every year."

Like most Baptist churches, this one is sparsely decorated. It has a mauve carpet, some brass chandeliers and two aisles of pews facing a raised choir loft at the top of the room. A plain wooden cross hangs on the centre of the otherwise bare wall. To its right is the Christian flag (a red cross on a blue and white background) and to the left the Stars and Stripes. There is no altar or tabernacle. The only similarities to a Catholic church are the pretty stained-glass windows. Most of the money here seems to be invested in the sound system, an elaborate console of buttons and knobs worthy of a rock concert.

The noise level began to rise as people of all ages arrived to fill the pews and choir loft. These were no suburban sweat-pant slouches. It was Friday night but everyone was formally dressed: men and boys in shirts and slacks, girls in skirts and heels, some homely, but most decked out in the latest big city styles. Stephen's father called the crowd to order and threw out some Bible trivia.

"The Bible uses the words 'sing' and 'song' two hundred and fifteen times. Music and musicians are mentioned seventy-four times and thirteen musical instruments are named in scripture."

"Amen," responded the three-hundred-strong congregation, as duelling pianists belted out a lively ragtime beat and in perfect harmony the chapel erupted into song. "Glory, Glory, Alleluia," they sang, children and young adults mixing it up together. Seated in a back pew, I felt the urge to sway or clap. But nobody else was; it was all quite reserved, with just a bit of foot-tapping here and there. The tempo accelerated as the singers continued with songs about making it to heaven like "Mansions Await" and "Homecoming in the Skies". I tried to follow along in the hymn book but could not keep up as they raced from one number to the next. After fifteen minutes of this, the choir switched to a slower set. This one must have been for the sinners because they sang "Tell Jesus on me" and bluntly warned that "You can run but you can't hide".

Nobody here seemed shy or nervous. A boy of about fourteen alternated between conducting the choir and playing piano before swapping seats with a girl who picked up the pace. In front of me a tiny baby was being rocked to the beat — too young to be born again, perhaps. Kelli Key, a brown-eyed girl whose face lit up as she sang, had come from Stockbridge, Georgia, about an hour's drive away. At twelve she's at the age at which most evangelical Christians who have grown up with the tradition can expect to go through a "born again" experience. But Kelli told me that she qualified for the early bird special; she was saved at age nine.

"How did you know?" I wanted to know.

"You just do. I lay in bed for several nights, thinking about it, but you can feel it. Then all you have to do is ask to be saved. Jesus comes knocking on your heart."

"What do you think the benefit of being saved is?" I asked.

"You can go to heaven," she replied simply, looking at me as if I should know this.

Kelli was happy, brimming with confidence, smiling and nodding to passing friends as she talked. It was as if she had been seized by the good fairy who had banished the usual pre-teen hang-ups about her weight or interacting with other people. "I just love coming here; I love the music and my dad sings too. He often stays up until midnight to sing with me and my brother," she enthused, making you understand that she couldn't ask for anything more than to be here with family by her side and Jesus knocking on her heart.

GETTING THE WHOLE FAMILY SAVED is an established evangelical tradition. But across America they are stepping beyond the hearth. According to a document released in 2005 by the National

Association of Evangelicals, God has given them "an awesome opportunity to shape public policy in ways that could contribute to the well-being of the entire world". This declaration comes at a time when rows over personal morality and religious references are raging all the way up to the United States Supreme Court. Even the Ten Commandments were put on trial in a case that argued over whether or not they could be displayed on government property. Groups in several states fought to keep the laws of God on display, but opponents argued that the American Constitution guarantees not to promote one religion over any other and that the Ten Commandments are clearly Christian. The irony is that the stone tablets found in many public buildings in America were placed there in the 1950s, not by Moses or by anyone claiming to represent him, but by the movie-maker Cecil B. De Mille as an advertisement for his epic of the same name. But that was back when America was still "one nation under God". In 2005 the Supreme Court ruled that one set of these stone tablets could be left on government land outside a public building in Texas, while another had to be removed from inside a courthouse in Kentucky.

The Bible Baptist church in Monroe faced its own challenge from the secular world when a gospel-singing event filmed for local television was cancelled because it featured the word "Jesus". Stephen laughed as he struggled to comprehend the silliness of it all.

"We stood up to them — had a face-to-face confrontation. We were probably seen as fundamentalist nuts but that's fine. I'll stand up for what I believe is right. The show ended up back on television." Even in small towns, he claimed, authorities scared of lawsuits are capitulating to the whims of individuals who want to banish Jesus and Christmas from the public square. "In New Jersey I heard they wouldn't let Christmas carols be sung. This is America, you can't do this here. As Christians we've got to stand up or we'll get pushed around," he added. The Christmas carols are only part of the story. Some Americans want Happy Christmas replaced by Happy Holidays and even argue that a nativity scene on government property needs to include reindeer to balance out the religious symbolism. If it has no reindeer, it has got to go, since it violates the separation of church and state.

Politics had no place at this singing weekend, however. This was about pianos and pizza and other small p's. But like other right-wing Christians across America, Stephen is happy that George Bush was re-elected President for a second term. Four out of five evangelicals voted for Mr Bush, a significant booster in an election that was running neck-and-neck until the very end. Stephen's church could not endorse either George Bush or John Kerry from the pulpit, but they could talk about issues like homosexuality and abortion and they did. Moreover, as private citizens Stephen and his father Pastor Greg Butler put Bush stickers on their cars and encouraged everyone they knew to vote for him.

"I think he has good eye contact. He looks people in the eye and he tells them the truth."

Like President Bush, Stephen Butler is very open to the possibility that much of what has happened in the world in the past few years has been preordained and that the Texan was put in the White House for a reason.

"For sure President Bush is in God's plan. The Bible says no nation rises or falls or kings don't come and go without the Lord knowing it. He set President Bush up for a reason. Bush is there because of God's mercy on America."

The young pastor is fearful, however, that after eight years of George Bush, Christian conservatives will rest on their laurels and lose out in the next presidential election. He is barely old enough to remember the Reagan era but says the same thing happened back then. Conservatives who supported Ronald Reagan went to sleep and, after one term of George Bush Sr, allowed the presidency to fall into the hands of the more liberal Bill Clinton. Stephen could be right. Just months into President George W. Bush's second term, some polls were showing that most

Americans would vote for Hillary Clinton over a Republican next time around. That's enough to put the fear of God in the Butlers and the Christian right. I asked Stephen if he agrees with everything President Bush has done.

"On most moral issues, I'm standing with him one hundred per cent," he answered, then paused and shook his head. "But I wish he would be more kind to Israel. Israel is God's chosen nation and I think he needs to do everything he can to facilitate it."

"Isn't his unwavering support for Israel part of the problem in the Middle East?" I enquired.

But Stephen is not interested in an unbiased approach to the conflict; his is the biblical approach. Evangelicals believe that only when the Jews return to Israel will Jesus come again to fulfil the "end of times" prophecies outlined in the Book of Revelations.

"He's trying to get them to give away land that God promised them. I think that's something he needs to wake up and change his mind on, because the Bible says in the last times people will be drawn back to Israel. They are already going back."

THESE GOSPEL-SINGING WEEKENDS are marathon events. After finishing up near eleven o'clock the previous night with performances from some aspiring Christian rock artists, everyone was seated and ready to begin again by ten the next morning. Stephen's father had brought a stack of CDs recorded by local gospel quartets for me to listen to on the way home, good wholesome music that sells as well as saves. I was still confused about the born again issue and asked Greg if being saved restrains a person from further sin. "Oh no, we all sin every day, that's why we need to be saved." He nodded slowly in that way Americans do as they watch you trying to process their words.

It's also very unclear how Jesus will pick his chosen few when he comes back. The Book of Revelations indicates that Jesus might take only one hundred and forty-four thousand souls away with him in the event known to evangelicals as the Rapture. This is when people will be selectively snatched from the earth and lifted up to heaven.

I tackled Kelli Key's older brother Ben on this one. The burly twenty-two-year-old looks as though he would be more at home in a wrestling ring than a church but he speaks softly and plays a mean piano without shape notes or any other notes to guide him. "The one hundred and forty-four thousand, that's a controversial subject," he confirmed. "There's a lot of different interpretations, but it says earlier in the Bible that all who believe will be saved. I believe if you accept Christ, you will be," he continued. Just four years out of high school, Ben owns his own construction company and would soon be marrying a girl from Stockbridge. I had seen them together the previous night. She was blonde and statuesque, genuine model material, but as she gazed dreamily at a friend's baby, it was clear that her ambition did not extend beyond motherhood and apple pie in rural Georgia. From what I could see, these young people had not been coerced into coming. They had consciously chosen faith and gospel music over a night on the town. "The world is full of music," smiled Ben Key, "but gospel is the only kind that has a message with it. You can listen to pop or rock but it's just a bunch of instruments."

Yet despite this seemingly simple devotion to the Bible and to getting to heaven, the term "evangelicals" has become a pejorative one. Europeans see them as right-wing maniacs and a large proportion of Americans, including believers, see a movement trying to forge an all-Christian nation intolerant of other faiths. This was reinforced when prominent evangelist Franklin Graham, son of Billy Graham, described the Muslim faith as "wicked" at the start of the Iraq war. Because they believe Jesus is the only way to the Father, evangelicals hold that Muslims, Buddhists or Hindus cannot be redeemed.

The modern evangelical movement in America surfaced in the 1940s when mainline Protestantism was at its height. Now, according to their national association, evangelicals are running far ahead of other denominations. Back in 1968, they had ten churches with congregations of over two and a half thousand people. Today there are nearly a thousand such mega-churches, with two more being added each week. Joel Osteen, a popular evangelical minister in Houston, hosts thirteen thousand people at his Sunday worship. He has to take over a sports arena to fit everyone in. There was a time when evangelicals could not get access to the airwaves, yet today they control ninety per cent of Christian broadcasting. One quarter of the two hundred and forty seminaries in the US are run by evangelical Christians. This growth has been a phenomenon of the suburbs and exurbs, the areas where white Americans settled in the 1960s and 1970s after deserting the cities. The black community is less evangelical; the movement ignored their civil rights struggle, a mistake it has regretted ever since. As with all religions, the fastest growth is taking place among immigrants. Asians have been quickly joining the ranks of the born again, and Latin Americans are thought to be switching from Catholicism to the evangelical camp at a rate of thousands a day. In America new converts are urban as well as suburban, vote Democrat as much as Republican, and are as likely to care about human rights, poverty and religious freedom abroad as they are about same-sex marriage or the state of Israel.

BACK IN MONROE, TRAINEE PASTOR Stephen Butler was mulling over the decline of faith in Europe where fewer than twenty per cent now attend church regularly, as opposed to over forty per cent in the US.

"It's sad," he reflected. "Sad when you consider that our main religion came from Europe." He assumed I was familiar with Charles Haddon Spurgeon, a pastor at the Metropolitan Baptist Tabernacle in London in the mid-nineteenth century, and asked if I had read about him. I hadn't. "You should," he urged. "People came to America to get away from religious oppression in Europe. Now we are sending missionaries back to convert people to Christ."

With more people turning to evangelism and Pentecostal worship, mainstream denominations are taking a big hit. Methodists, Lutherans, Episcopalians and, to an extent, Catholics cannot compete with churches where everything from amplified music and dancing and speaking in tongues can all be part of the worship. There is another theory that says the old churches don't ask enough from their congregants and that those that demand more money and more personal restraint actually do a better job of holding on to their members. Fundamentalist groups who deny themselves alcohol, certain foods and smutty television have been growing, while those relying on voluntary self-discipline are emptying out. And then there is the social aspect of church-going in America. With people often moving from state to state, the church is where they find like-minded friends. Non-traditional churches appear to be winning this game too, often doubling up as semi-private social clubs.

As the weekend wrapped up, Stephen was satisfied that the gospel-singing tradition is in safe hands for now. He was not nearly so hopeful about America's future.

"The Genesis story of Sodom and Gomorrah, it's so similar to America. The sexual immorality. It's everywhere here."

Evangelicals have no tolerance for homosexuality and promote abstinence as a way to avoid teenage pregnancies and abortions. But despite the efforts of the evangelical movement to drag America out of its iniquitous cesspit, Stephen doesn't necessarily expect good things for the country. And he had news for me.

"God's Word doesn't mention America, not one time that I can see," he said, looking me in the eye. Russia and China, he pointed out, are mentioned in the Bible, as are Israel and the Middle East. "But America? I don't see it there."

"What do you think that means?" I asked, almost afraid of what was coming next.

"I don't think America is going to stand as she once did, there's too much fault at the top, too much corruption. I'm not saying she will be totally and utterly destroyed but my hopes are not in America. My hopes are in the Lord."

"How does that work?"

"We look for Christ to come back and get us. That's what I'm waiting for."

Barely into his twenties, Stephen is cooling his heels until everything ends. And there will be no warning from above. The Bible says, "Watch therefore, for ye know not what hour your Lord doth come". The Rapture, evangelicals believe, will be either followed or accompanied by a great Tribulation — storms, wars and earthquakes that will destroy those left behind. As he waits, Stephen will continue to spread the word, sing songs and help save more souls while there's still time. That weekend, I drove away from the town of Monroe with a lot to think about and something I needed to buy: a Bible.

Chapter 4

The Simple Life

THE TWO-YEAR-OLD BOY sitting beside me at the dinner table was glancing around furtively to see if anyone had seen what he had just done. He decided they had not, so again, when he thought the coast was clear, he knelt up on his chair, stretched out and dug a finger deep into the dish of peanut butter. Then he sat back down and slowly licked the sweet sticky mixture off his hand — quite a daring feat to perform in front of eighteen strangers sitting around the table who had come to observe him.

Maylan Jr is normal in all respects, maybe a little small for his age but healthy and bright. Dressed in tiny navy overalls and a blue shirt, with his straight blond hair falling about his ears, he is what the Americans call "cute". Judging by his ability to empty the peanut butter dish without igniting a firestorm, he also exemplifies the other meaning of the word. A disapproving glance from his mother was received and understood momentarily but soon was trumped by the thrill of fooling her while she was otherwise occupied.

But there are certain truths about Maylan Stoltzfus Jr. He will probably never ride a bicycle, never wear a pair of Nike runners, never watch a movie nor attend university. Not because he can't, but because, as a member of an Old Order Amish family, it's highly likely that he will never want to.

I met Maylan and his family at their farm near the town of Intercourse, Pennsylvania — for me, one of the most bucolic settings in America. At the arrival of spring, the fields rolled across the landscape like deep-pile carpets, light brown where the mineral-rich soil had been newly ploughed, green where the first of the alfalfa crop was emerging after two days of rain. In the distance a lime-coloured strip of newly mown grass added light and warmth to the picture.

The Stoltzfus farm is set well back from the road and is as peaceful as a sleepy Sunday. Clustered around the main house are a barn and outhouses, all dwarfed by two shiny storage elevators whose rounded tops reflect the patterns of the sky. The buildings are large but plain and as neat as a new pin. At the side of the house are an immaculately manicured rock garden and raised vegetable beds planted with peas and carrots. The whole scene is a study in tidiness; the only clue that five young children live here is a small plastic tractor and a basketball hoop. As the sun departed there was no sound apart from the shifting of some dairy cows in a pen.

"The light needs more air pumped into it." Maylan Sr, the boys' father, apologised for the fading light as he unhooked the kerosene lamp hanging over the dinner table. "It's thirteen years old, so I suppose it needs an overhaul." He left the kitchen, returning moments later with the light burning brightly again. Apart from two lamps, each whining like boiling kettles, there is no other source of light in the Stoltzfus house. That's how they like it. Because of the ways of the Old Order Church, the Amish don't use electricity and are forbidden to have any wiring in the house which connects them to the outside world. Our supper of fried chicken and homemade sausage came courtesy of a propane gas cooker — a small nod towards modernity. Maylan's wife Barbie, a small but sturdy-looking woman, spoke with an almost Irish lilt as she explained that she likes to cook for "English" — their term for those outside of the Amish community. On this particular night she had invited a group to dinner for a small fee. Aside from supplementing the family income, it's an opportunity to educate the outside world about the Amish lifestyle. Her four boys — Lester who is twelve, Melvin aged nine, Marvin who is six years old and Maylan Jr — were all supposed to be helping her. Her daughter Lillian, who was not feeling well, had gone to her room somewhere in the darkened house.

WHEN YOU ARRIVE IN AMISH COUNTRY, you are forced to check your sense of time and speed. Gradually the noise and bustle of the "English" world dissolves, leaving an uncommon serenity. It takes time to adjust as you pass the multitude of tourist attractions that clog the small towns of Bird-in-Hand and Intercourse. Initially it can seem as though you have entered a trap designed to inveigle visitors into emptying their wallets in quaint quilt and furniture shops. Even the shadowy figures with their long beards and dark attire seem contrived at first glance. But when you leave the villages behind and drive along the back roads of Lancaster County, it becomes clear that this is not for show. Immediately you feel the pace shift downwards and involuntarily lift your foot off the accelerator and switch off the car radio. To do otherwise would be to disrespect the silence of those living their American dream of a life without haste or convenience.

Almost three centuries after their arrival from Europe in a small group of a few hundred, there are now about one hundred and fifty thousand Americans living the Amish lifestyle — twenty-five thousand of them in this corner of Pennsylvania. The Amish are descendants of the sixteenth-century Anabaptists, a religious group formed in Europe. "Anabaptist" means to be opposed to the practice of infant baptism. As they see it people should join a church when they are young adults and in a position to reject or accept membership for themselves. The original Anabaptists were the Mennonites, followers of a former Catholic priest called Menno Simons, but in 1693 in Switzerland, a new group called the Amish split from the Mennonites, claiming the latter had become too lax in enforcing certain rules. The Amish believed that errant or lapsed church members needed to be shunned until they had repented and come back into compliance with the strict rules that govern how they live. Like many groups remaining outside of the mainstream European religions of the time, the Amish suffered persecution and in the eighteenth century some moved to the United States. They settled on farmland in Ohio, Illinois, Missouri, Nebraska and in Pennsylvania, where William Penn's experiment in religious tolerance had begun. Eventually they too disagreed over rules on how to live their lives and split into a number of smaller groups, including the New Order Amish and Beachy Amish, who are more liberal than the Old Order.

Unlike many other religious Americans, the Amish do not talk openly about their devotion or issues of doctrine. They do not pick fights with other religious groups over what they believe, and they do not proselytise. They choose instead to live their faith by the example of their lives. While based on the Bible and the teachings of Jesus Christ, their beliefs are made real by keeping old traditions and by refusing to get caught up in the haste and craziness of the modern world.

The Bible tells them, in 1 John 2:15: "Love not the world, neither the things that are in the world. If any man love the world, the love of the Father is not in him."

Amish faith demands humility. Individualism is not encouraged. It's all about the community. Everybody dresses in the same dark, plain-coloured clothes. A girl is supposed to be buried in the same outfit she is married in: a simple blue dress, the length of which is often dictated by the local church. Hairstyles are uniform:

drawn back in a bun and worn under a prayer cap for the women; long around the ears or just below the rim of the hat for the men. Pockets are forbidden since they could be used for carrying worldly goods that might set one member apart from the others; and buttons, which are considered a sign of pride, are replaced by simple hooks and eyes. The girls wear no makeup or jewels — all they are permitted to show off are their youthful clear complexions.

"English" discover quickly that the Amish don't like having their photograph taken, believing that images of themselves are a sign of vanity. On a previous visit to Amish country I learned the hard way about these private and deeply reticent people. Spotting a group tilling a field, I climbed over the fence and, armed with a radio recording machine, began by requesting interviews. About a dozen of them, all men, just stood in silence looking at me. I explained that I was from Ireland and just wanted to ask them about their unique lifestyle, but again there was no response and the men resumed their work. I began to wonder if they didn't understand English, so I walked over to the oldest-looking of the bunch and, speaking more slowly and loudly, asked, "Are you in charge here?" "We don't have time to talk; we are working," he replied in perfect English before turning his back on me. I apologised profusely and scarpered back across the fence.

That night I recounted my futile trip into the cornfield to the owner of the house where I was staying. He told me that I might have stood a better chance had I been properly dressed. Looking me up and down, he suggested that wearing a crocheted top with holes all over it was not the best way to start a conversation with these humble people. This time I made sure I packed a long skirt and cardigan!

THE OLD ORDER AMISH have also removed themselves from the outside world by their attitude to transport. Self-propelled vehicles are forbidden by most groups and even rubber tyres are banned — ruling out bicycles.

"It's not that we think a bicycle is evil or nothing," explained Maylan Stoltzfus; "it's just that they can go too far and too fast."

Over the course of a few days I saw several youngsters zipping around the roads on scooters that moved as fast as any bicycle but the physical energy needed to keep up the pace would still limit a journey to a few miles. A bike would be more likely to take them all the way to Philadelphia, which to an Amish youngster would be like reaching Europe; most have never seen the nearest big town. Instead of cars, the Amish still use horse-drawn carriages with steel wheels. The distinctive grey buggies are a common sight on the roads of Lancaster County, and the "clip-clop-clip-clop" sound remains with you long after you leave. Even at close quarters, the enclosed carriages seem barely big enough to carry one passenger, but you can count up to four heads inside as they pass by.

As the pace of life around the edges of Lancaster County has picked up and new development has encroached, the roads have become death traps for these people and their horses. Having to compete for road space with all manner of cars and trucks, accidents are commonplace. It is not unusual to see impatient drivers aggressively overtaking the buggies without any regard for the safety of those travelling inside. In most states, the Old Order Amish have been forced by the courts to display flashing lights and reflectors on the buggies, for safety. They had fiercely resisted this change but, being part of the larger American community, they are bound to obey the law of the land. "You can't change the outside world," reflected Maylan, who travels everywhere by horse and buggy with Barbie and the children. "You have to accept it and work with it."

Though this antiquated mode of transport comes in a limited variety of makes and models and in just one colour, it plays the same role for the Amish teenage boy as the car does for his "English" counterpart. On turning sixteen he is given his own buggy for the purpose of dating. With more liberties available to the young, he can decorate the inside of his "courting buggy" with feathers and love hearts and even a stereo, but once he marries, the decorations and the music have to go — forever. Since his reach along the great American highway is limited, any girlfriend is generally from the local area. Inter-church marriage is forbidden but, with the sustained growth in the Old Order communities, there are still plenty of Amish partners to choose from.

"I met Barbie when I was eighteen and she was sixteen," recalled Maylan, depositing a jug of cool mint tea on the dinner table together with more mouth-watering fried chicken. "I didn't ask her out for about six months after that."

Living ten miles apart — well over an hour's journey by horse and buggy — had been a hindrance, but he had managed to visit her a few times. "She said 'yes' and the rest followed from there."

Barbie, who appeared stern and shy up to this, began to laugh as he recounted their story. She has a pleasant face and surprisingly large hands that have the look of physical work about them. Her husband is tall and well-built with piercing eyes, a long jet-black beard and a pudding-bowl haircut. He has an easy way with people and does most of the talking to the dinner group. Now aged thirty-four and thirty-six, Barbie and Maylan have been married for thirteen years and have five children, but there's no indication from either that they are finished with five. Barbie is the eldest of thirteen children and Maylan has eight siblings.

As they expressed their feelings about the life they have chosen, they seemed intensely proud that they have upheld their traditions and their disciplines.

Barbie and her boys speak to one another in a language called Pennsylvania Dutch which is a German dialect brought from Europe. Although all Amish learn and speak English well, it is the language of their ancestors that is used to communicate in the home. "It's not German but it's close," Maylan explained, joking that they probably wouldn't starve if they had to move to Germany. He and Barbie feel lucky to be among the last of the Amish who will be to able set up farms in this area. There is no more land.

Maylan was given his thirty-two acres by his father, who in turn had split a larger piece of land with his father before him. But with couples having an average of seven children, farming is now a realistic option for just one child — generally the youngest son. The rest have to diversify into trades like woodworking or welding. Some Amish have taken jobs outside the community, restoring antiques and building mobile homes. Of Maylan's family of nine, only two are farming. The rest of the boys are welding, trained by their father and grandfather who saw the land crisis coming.

Every available acre of land in Lancaster County has already been snapped up by the Amish. Elaine Lahr, who runs a local bed and breakfast in a pretty brick house among the Amish farms, recalled her experience of bidding against Amish buyers at a house auction. "I stopped bidding when I had gone fifty thousand dollars over what I wanted to pay. They bid way above what the place was worth and they paid in cash," she told me.

Lancaster is the oldest Amish settlement in the US and the most affluent. Though the ubiquitous clotheslines, which display washing for armies of children, give an impression of poverty, most Amish are thriving. They just don't use drying machines! They don't use credit cards either, relying mainly on cash for all business transactions. They refuse to sue over disputes and don't believe in buying insurance. If things go wrong, it is deemed to be God's will and problems are resolved by the community which rallies around the stricken family. Despite a clean-living lifestyle that forbids drinking alcohol or smoking, they get sick like anyone else. Heart disease, cancers, arthritis, mental disorders and depression are commonplace. Without insurance, they try to avoid the overpriced American medical system and, according to Elaine Lahr, busloads of the Amish frequently travel up into Canada for medical treatment.

MENNO, A BEARDED MAN who looks fifteen years older than his forty years, has been driving tourists around in a horse-drawn buggy to support his wife and four children, one of whom is ill. For nine years he had been woodworking but that had gone quiet, so he had switched to the business of describing his lifestyle to the hordes of tourists who come through here every year with their mouths and wallets open. "You do what you have to do," he told me, giving the impression that it's a bit of a chore having to explain over and over again to outsiders why the Amish don't watch television and have never heard of Britney Spears or U2.

"Look, there's one of our one-room school houses." He points, probably for the umpteenth time today, to a small structure on a hill. It is not unlike some rural Irish schools. Amish children are privately educated for eight years from age six until fourteen. Their elders see no practical purpose in spending any longer at books, since the extra hands will be needed on the farm and in the kitchen as soon as they become strong enough. Students like Barbie's sons Lester and Melvin study reading, writing and arithmetic. They are taught not by public school teachers but by one of their own who is judged suitable for the role of teacher. Normally a young woman, the teacher will have no more than eight years of education herself. In the 1970s the practice of pulling children from school at fourteen was debated in the United States Supreme Court. Opponents claimed that American law required every child to be educated to a certain level, but the court decided that the Amish should not be punished because they were different and upheld their right to educate their children as they saw fit.

"We do our homework in school," explained Lester, the eldest of the Stoltzfus boys, when I enquired if he had any lessons to do. He and his younger brother Melvin both seem bookish. Melvin was curled up on the couch near a second kerosene lamp with a book and a peanut butter sandwich. Twelve-year-old Lester, a puny lad who peers out from behind a pair of Harry Potter-like spectacles, will be leaving school in two years' time, first to help at home and then to be trained for a trade. If he has any dreams of becoming a doctor or a scientist, he will have to keep them to himself.

The rest of America began to leave this simple life behind about a hundred and fifty years ago. First came the rubber tyre which got everyone moving more quickly, then mechanisation allowing tasks to be completed faster and by fewer hands. Now in America, as in much of the western world, more and more people are employed in the service and information industries, sitting in front of computer screens with no physical end product. The majority has moved to crowded cities or purpose-built commuter towns and few would know how to feed or clothe themselves without supermarkets and shopping malls. Television is the prism through which American culture and the world abroad is viewed and the media focuses not on slowing down or going back to basics but on ever newer, bigger, faster and more efficient technologies.

I was surprised to learn that the Amish have their own media and journalists, with the old-fashioned biblical title of "scribes". In a shop in Intercourse, I picked up their paper, *Die Botschaft*, for fifty cents and read for several hours, gleaning more information about people's real lives than I have ever got from the *New York Times* or the *Washington Post*. Instead of articles focusing on specific issues or concerns, *Die Botschaft*, which means "the messenger", is a series of daily diaries from Amish families in several American states. Take this despatch from Milroy, Pennsylvania:

> Greetings in our Saviour's name. This date is the 28th birthday of cousin Jesse J. Hostleter. Today was windy. Yesterday, Sunday, was snowy and blustery. Saturday it rained about all day. . . . Dads and I were away on errands this evening. I spent some time grafting trees at uncles Jesse's. Met Seth Hostleter of East Milroy district on the road. Seth had a mishap a week ago Sunday, when on the way to church their horse scared from something along the road. The horse went into a fence, Seth had his face bruised and is still black around the eyes.

The news from Allensville, Pennsylvania, is more upbeat:

A cheery greeting to all readers. I'm beginning my day's work in the greenhouse. It's greening up so fast, real soon now we'll need to move the petunias outside . . . baby boy was born to brother Thomas and Lena on Monday. Believe this is number thirteen and he's named Emmanuel. That makes ninety-one grands for Dads.

Then there are the weekly notices like this one from a Mrs King:

Did anyone get the wrong hat at Amos and Sarann's wedding in March? Alvin's wasn't there when he went to get it so he came home without one. It's almost new and has his initials in, AJK.

Contained in these simple diaries was all the news that's fit to print: births, deaths, accidents and illnesses, the weather and even lost hats. And the reference to ninety-one grands for Dads did mean what I thought it did: little Emmanuel was indeed the ninety-first grandchild for someone in Allensville.

"How many cousins do you have?" I asked Barbie Stoltzfus as she dished out shoofly pie, an Amish staple made from molasses, marshmallow and brown sugar. She thought for a while before answering: "Probably about eighty-five on my side, and about sixty on Maylan's — that's about one hundred and forty between us." A gasp went around the table and, just to prove that she was not joking, Barbie disappeared and arrived back with the obituary for Maylan's grandfather, Roy Stoltzfus, who had passed away the previous August aged ninety, leaving seventy-eight grandchildren and two hundred great-grandchildren after him.

"Number two hundred was born the day before he died and another arrived the day he was buried, making two hundred and one," she elaborated.

SUCH A LARGE CROWD may be tough when it comes to remembering birthdays but the sense of togetherness in Amish families is the envy of people the world over. In refusing to accept even the initial stages of the Industrial Revolution, they have sacrificed speed and convenience for community. Because they don't migrate much, people like Barbie and Maylan live just a few miles away from their siblings and, with so many relatives around, no one ever wants for anything. There is always a sister or a cousin available to help with child-minding, or harvesting crops, or raising a barn that has burned down. Huge cowsheds have been rebuilt and made ready for milking just two days after a fire.

As with their schools, the Old Order Amish don't attend an institutionalised church but hold church gatherings in their homes on every second Sunday. The community is divided into districts, each with about twenty-five families. Church service is rotated among the homes in the district.

"It comes around here about every seven or eight months," Barbie explained, pointing out that the sliding doors in the large kitchen give way to an adjoining room, creating space for about one hundred and fifty people. Church is not open to outsiders and is held in High German, a language different from Pennsylvania Dutch. From what little is known, services are conducted with men in one room and women in the other with the preacher standing in the doorway between the two rooms. Elders sit at the front and young men at the back. The teenagers remove their hats and file in to their seats under the watchful eyes of the girls in the other room. At the service, which lasts about three hours from eight in the morning until eleven, selected scriptures are read and hymns are sung *a cappella* from the *Ausband,* a book of Christian hymns unchanged since the fifteenth century. The tunes are passed on orally through the generations. Visiting elders from other districts or even from other states are welcomed to these gatherings but the key clerical figure is the bishop, a local man appointed to be the guardian of the doctrine or the *Ordnung* — the set of rules which governs Amish faith.

"We draw lots for the bishops." Menno the buggy driver explained that bits of straw are placed inside Bibles and all a man has to do to become a bishop is to take up the correct Bible from a stack on the floor. After talking to several people, I got the feeling that not many Amish men covet the responsibility of being bishop. He has to decide what lifestyle changes can and cannot be introduced in the community, often under great pressure to allow change for the sake of prosperity. Elaine Lahr recalled being urged by an Amish woman who worked for her to petition the district bishop for a bicycle. She had wanted special dispensation to ride the bicycle to and from work, a journey of several miles. Rather than bring up such a potentially explosive topic, Elaine had assured the woman that she would pick her up and leave her home each day. While her Amish employee could not ride a bicycle or drive a car, she could, in the interests of practicality, be driven around by a non-Amish person.

The bishops have spent much of their time in recent years deliberating on the issue of telephones. Because phones connect the home to the outside world by means of wires, they are forbidden, but most farmers and businessmen have now been allowed to install a phone out in a barn or in a shared booth on the roadside. Some of the younger Amish, according to Elaine Lahr, are even using mobile phones, a major contradiction, but one which slips by the strict rules — because mobiles are not connected by wires. Some Amish furniture-makers and craftsmen now have websites to advertise their products. While they themselves may never log on to a computer or may never have even seen one, if an outsider sets up the site, the Amish can partake of this most modern of technologies. Construction contractors working away from home are allowed to use certain machines, and diesel engines have become commonplace on farms. The bishops feel that these improvements do not betray their faith.

THE AMISH DON'T BAPTISE their children into the church, but baptism is a major consideration for young adults. When they turn seventeen, they are ostensibly allowed to decide for themselves if they want to join the Old Order. Most are offered the opportunity and are often encouraged to go away and taste what they will be missing once they commit to the church. This period of exploration is called *Rumspringa*. Many do try out big city life or take the opportunity to travel. Girls swap their plain dresses for bikinis on the beach and often develop romantic relationships that would be frowned upon back home. In 2004, an American reality television series raised plenty of Amish eyebrows when it tracked a group of youngsters as they discovered the world beyond the barn door. Those less inclined to venture to the cities stay closer to home for their period of investigation but are free to drive cars, drink alcohol or do whatever they want so long as it's legal. The amazing result of this seemingly risky experiment is that, in the twenty-first century, with so much to distract young people from tradition, eighty per cent of young Amish formally decide to enter the church. In some communities the figure is as high as one hundred per cent.

"When they commit to the church, the young people seem even more disciplined than the generations before them," claimed Elaine Lahr, who has been visiting or living in Lancaster County for forty years. Whether they feel ill-equipped for the world outside or whether they just don't care for it, most feel they have too much to lose by leaving the fold.

"Parents hope that their kids would stay in the church," Maylan Stoltzfus confirmed as we finish dinner. He had not bothered venturing out to see America as a young lad. "I knew I wanted to stay," he told me without a hint of regret over what a bright, affable, good-looking man might have missed on the outside.

I attempted to dig deeper. "What is it out there that you would not want for your children?"

He laughed loudly and with his arms folded shot me a knowing look. "There's a lot out there I don't want for my children. I don't have to tell you there's a lot out there you probably wouldn't want for yours either." Some of the other visitors around the table, mainly tourists from New York to the north and Maryland to the south, were nodding in agreement. "There's plenty we don't want for our teenagers," one woman repeated, sounding as though she would like to impose some Amish discipline on her own family.

Maylan could not name a single thing he is missing by living away from the mainstream. "I like it here," he told me several times as we chatted about farming and animals and the future, which seems to get more difficult with every passing year. Just miles from the Amish settlement, discount shopping outlets have sprung up, their very presence an affront to the frugal lifestyle practised there. "You can't fight progress, you just do what you can," Maylan added, saying that the important thing is to maintain unity among the community and the district.

Tourism is welcome but it brings traffic congestion and the feeling of living in a fishbowl. Intriguing icons the Amish may be, but sometimes they would prefer to be left alone. After all, freedom to live and worship as you please is what America is about. Since coming to America, this freedom has allowed the Amish to flourish but, like everywhere, it has its price. Maylan feels that if all lifestyle changes were to be blocked by the community elders, there could be an internal uprising and no one would stay. Small, slow, incremental changes, he thinks, are better than no change at all.

BY NOW HIS YOUNG BOYS were inside the door selling welded letter-holders and quilted oven gloves — souvenirs for the tourists to take back down the dizzying American highway. None of the Amish I met in Lancaster County pretended to know much about the happenings of that world. That weekend, CNN had been incessantly broadcasting the story of a runaway bride in Georgia but clearly nobody around there seemed to know about it. Some, however, do read newspapers, and several of the Old Order I met in Intercourse knew all about George Bush and had even voted for him.

"Because he's a Christian," explained Menno, driving his horse and trap past farmers' signs advertising fresh eggs and root beer for sale.

Mr Bush had courted the Amish vote by paying a visit to Lancaster County before his re-election.

"He came up Route 340 here; we were all watching out — the roads were closed and all. But he went by so fast in the bus. I wished he would have stopped. I could have taken him for a ride."

Menno chuckles as he collects his ten dollars apiece for the jaunt. The Amish are against war and during times of military drafts they have refused to get involved, yet many of the men voted for George Bush regardless of the wars in Iraq and Afghanistan.

"I don't know if I did the right thing or not, I don't know much about it but I like the way he handles things, he stays the course," said Menno, adding: "If I had him here, I'd ask him to reduce the cost of propane and food."

Menno's four children have never even been to Lancaster City, twenty miles away. "I'd like to take them to the Philadelphia Zoo some day," he pondered, as if this might be something requiring years of planning.

He did not seem optimistic that the Amish way of life could be sustained in Pennsylvania and seemed to be searching for a way out. "We thought God might come before the children grew up," he reflected.

"You mean the end of times?" I enquired.

"Yeah, everything is moving so fast now," he said, figuring that the world must surely be coming to its natural end. This "end of times" mentality is similar to what evangelicals believe, though the Amish don't talk of the Rapture or Armageddon. The Amish look forward to heaven but, unlike evangelicals, they only *hope* to be saved. To assume that they will certainly be saved, they feel, is conceited and individualistic.

Maylan Stoltzfus, who gives the Bible pride of place in his living room, also voted for George Bush but could not really explain why. He had never voted for anyone before.

"We hope for a God-fearing President," he told me finally, but silenced me by adding that he can do more by praying for the American President than getting involved in discussions about politics.

As for his own family, he was not prepared to look into their future on this spring evening in Pennsylvania.

"You don't know what it's going to be like in twenty or thirty years' time. You have to take it as it comes," he repeated for the third time, as we shook hands and parted.

THE FOLLOWING DAY THE RELATIVE BUSTLE of Saturday was gone and the whole place seemed sound asleep. No Amish business is done on the Sabbath and all shops were shut. At eight in the morning, two dozen buggies were lined up outside an Amish farm close to Elaine Lahr's bed and breakfast, where local families had gathered for church. From outside the house you couldn't hear a sound, no singing or chanting or laughing or arguing. But I could picture the woman of the house counting out shoofly pies and smothering bread with creamy peanut butter and apple sauce for the refreshments. I wondered who might be looking for a telephone or some other convenience which they could sneak past the Old Order rules. Three hours later, with church finished, I noticed young boys in their Sunday suits and straw hats rollerblading along the roads — another step away from the past.

In spite of creeping threats to their lifestyle, though, the Old Order population continues to grow steadily. As land has become scarce, they have spread out to as many as twenty-four states. With large families and loyal children, this is actually one of the fastest-growing religions anywhere.

"If they could just lift up the whole place and transport it to the middle of Ohio, I think they would," reflected Elaine Lahr's husband John. There are few places left in America's burgeoning North-east which can provide the isolation necessary for the church to thrive.

As I drove away from the rolling fields of green and brown and lime, leaving the neat farms and shining elevators behind, I could sense that I was already moving too fast. For three days I had slowed down to the pace of the Amish, and now revving up again felt so unnatural. But where I was going, speed and hurry was necessary for my very survival. Back out on Route I-95, the main highway from Maine to Florida, sticking to the sixty miles per hour speed limit could actually be dangerous. A slowcoach could cause an accident where everyone else was doing eighty or ninety.

Chapter 5

The Red Sea

*I*T HAS BEEN CLEAR FOR SOME TIME that America is split in half: two
nations inhabited by two radically different varieties of human
being. On the one hand there is the outward-looking, modern,
Democratic America which ruled the roost for most of the last four
decades, and on the other hand there is the traditionalist, God-
fearing, largely Republican America now enjoying its day in the
sun. Perhaps it's something in the water. The first America, often
referred to as "blue", is situated along the coasts in New York, the
New England states and California, as well as in patches along the
Mississippi River and around the Great Lakes. Red America covers
the rest of the country. That's most of the South, the Heartland,
the West and the Midwest — the parts most European visitors
rarely see on their way from New York to LA.

These days it's hard to pick out the tiny blue enclaves from the
sea of red. Yet because most of the larger cities are still blue, the
two varieties of Americans remain almost evenly divided. The

extent of this split was reinforced in both the 2000 and 2004 presidential elections, when red America and blue America fought to the finish in almost even matches. Since then, their differences of opinion on everything from war to religion to tastes in food and cars have continued to drive them apart. Instead of trying to get along, America's largely liberal coastal elite and its salt-of-the-earth populists have been deepening their dislike of one another with every passing day. What's really got them upset with each other, however, is the President. Blue America practically disowns its leader, but red America is Bush country.

Not everyone who voted for George Bush goes to church twice a week or quotes liberally from the Bible. Some prefer to spend Sunday at the motor speedway, watching their hometown heroes drive in circles around a track. Like any stereotype or label that is deemed to be politically incorrect, parlay it into comedy or satire, and it becomes trendy. Suddenly, black comedians and hip-hop stars are referring to themselves as "niggers", and rural, beer-drinkin', burger-eatin', Bush-votin' NASCAR fans are proud to be called "rednecks". For a close-up look at red Americans at play, a NASCAR race is the place to be.

NASCAR, which stands for "North American Stock Car Auto Racing", is the fastest-growing sport in the US, with an estimated seventy-five million followers. Though its appeal is spreading, its base is in southern red states like Alabama, Tennessee, the Carolinas and Virginia. A full month before the Chevy American Revolution 400 event at the Richmond International speedway in Virginia, all one hundred and ten thousand tickets were sold out, even though the cheap seats cost eighty dollars apiece. After some internet surfing and a batch of phone calls, I located a resale agent two thousand miles away in Phoenix, Arizona, who agreed to sell me tickets for a fifty per cent markup.

The enormity of the event did not dawn on me until I was driving south through Virginia on race day. The traffic just froze. There were still thirty miles to go to Richmond and several hours to the evening race. But judging by the gridlock, half of red America was trying to get there. The other half had arrived the previous day and had already constructed temporary accommodations, stretching for miles in every direction from the track. However, NASCAR is about cars, and being stuck in traffic is all part of the fun. In pickup trucks to my left and right, the party had already started. Moving at less than ten miles per hour, people were popping cans of beer and checking out one another's licence plates, some from as far north as Alaska or as far south as Louisiana.

It was hard to spot a truck that did not sport one of the sticky yellow ribbons that had flooded America since the beginning of the war in Iraq. In red America, being seen to support the troops is considered a solemn duty. As time has passed, though, enthusiasm for the war itself has eroded. Decades earlier the same distinction had been made during the Vietnam War where many Americans continued to support those doing the fighting while criticising the cause they were fighting for. The big difference then is that soldiers were drafted, often against their will. So far at least, those serving in the war on terror are all volunteers.

Slowly, we inched through a black neighbourhood where the residents had decided to remain indoors. Just one woman sat on her front porch, staring suspiciously at the trundling traffic. Richmond, a southern city, has a big population of African Americans, but she was the last black person I saw that day. Motor racing is a white sport. NASCAR hearkens back to the days when illegal alcohol distillers skilfully and speedily outran the law.

"It began as moonshine running. That's where the original racers came from. It used to be just the South. Now it's all over," a regular attender explained to me.

One of the sport's pioneers was Junior Johnson, a North Carolina farmer who, in his haste to deliver his illicit whiskey to Charlotte, figured out how to "make the motors fast and make the cars drive good". By the 1930s and 1940s, moonshiners were holding informal competitions on dirt tracks to see who had the fastest car. As descendants of the Scots-Irish, these men were also the first rednecks — their pale white skin turning red and leathery after years of working out in the sun.

The modern "redneck" is still either an outdoors man or a manual labourer. Plumbers, builders, farmers, workers and the guys who install cable TV all fit the mould. Stereotypically, he is the opposite of the coastal sophisticate, favouring a night in front of the TV with a few beers over an evening at the symphony. He has rarely been on public transport, preferring to drive himself around with the dog and kitchen sink in the back of the pickup and the gun in the rack. Politically he may come from a Democratic background but in 2000 and 2004 the all-American white male voted for George Bush in large numbers.

In fact, in recent years, motor-racing fans have been identified by election strategists as a new demographic, known as "NASCAR Dads". Replacing the "Soccer Moms" — those busy housewives who chose Bill Clinton in the 1990s — "NASCAR Dads" are those simple no-nonsense Bush folks who think the last line of the national anthem is "Gentlemen, start your engines!"

Why they want someone like Bush as President is a complicated question. They are mainly skilled or semi-skilled workers who have seen their jobs disappear and their wages stagnate since Bush came into office. They like lower taxes, but it's the rich who have benefited most from President Bush's tax cuts. Some are small farmers, yet Republican policies support huge agribusinesses that threaten their livelihoods. One factor seems to be that they are attracted by a conservative social agenda and are fully engaged in the culture war.

But the most likely answer is that they like George Bush because they see him as one of themselves. "He's a good man" and "He's got principles and stands for something" were the constant refrains from people I met in rural America. Bush is seen as an uncomplicated, black-and-white, right-and-wrong guy. The other attraction is that red Americans are the marrying type, and George

Bush values marriage. In almost every speech, he gives top billing to his wife Laura, and still gets a cheer every time he says "I married well". He knows this works. In all the red states, married couples now account for the majority of voters. States where single people are in the majority are the blue, Democrat-voting ones.

But red America may also be angry with the Democrats, concluding that the party has neglected its working-class base and is kowtowing to more affluent and left-leaning university graduates. This aversion to the intellectual elite, now associated with Democrats, was brought home to me time and time again on my travels.

"We're the ones who feed and clothe them, but they think they can tell us how to live our lives," one farmer said of his fellow Americans, as though he was referring to some unbearable enemy. Kay O'Connor, a teacher I met at a school in Kansas, talked of New York as if it were Satan's very own play pit. She would never move there and hoped that New Yorkers would not move to Kansas either. As a teacher in a private Catholic school, she felt her main role as an educator was to shield her students from the tide of liberalism threatening to destroy their values. O'Connor didn't hate anybody; she just didn't want people with different lifestyles or beliefs invading her territory.

CLOSER NOW TO THE RICHMOND SPEEDWAY, I found myself deep in "Dale" territory. The name was everywhere, on cars and t-shirts and tattooed on forearms. Dale Earnhardt is one of the most revered names in the history of American motor racing. From North Carolina, just below Richmond, Dale Earnhardt Sr dominated the sport for years before being tragically killed during a race in 2001. His son Dale Jr is now trying to inherit the mantle, but he seems to have conquered the merchandise racks rather than the track.

I eventually found a parking spot in a field which resembled a giant beach with no sand. For miles in every direction, racing fans had set up mini holiday camps out of the backs of their trucks. There were awnings and tents to sit under, tables for card games, gas canisters and portable grills for cooking. Some settlers had erected American or Confederate flags over their patches of grass, and country music blared from car radios. This pre-game ritual of staking out a spot and making it habitable is what the Americans call tailgating. And this was tailgate city.

Being a rookie tailgater, I had no patio furniture, no beer and no burgers. I was already melting in my jeans, and I had come in a Toyota truck, one of the very few foreign cars in this America-first sea of Fords, Dodges and Chevys.

"I was driving a Saab until last year," a man from outside Washington DC confided, indicating that this was sure to mark you out as an impostor from blue America. "I no longer drive a foreign car in here," he said. He had a passing interest in the race, but his principal motive in coming was to show his teenage son a different slice of American life. "We feel like renaissance men today. We even brought our barbecue with us," he grinned.

The hardcore fans do this almost every weekend during the racing season. And it didn't take long to find a crew who were intimately familiar with every racetrack in the country.

"Yep. Bristol, Dover, Martinsville. Done 'em all!" boasted Bruce from West Virginia, literally foaming at the mouth as he took another swig from a beer can. He had his top off, displaying a scrawny white torso and a farmer's tan — just on the neck and arms. "I'm forty years old, and I've been with it since the Billy Elliot days," he added, slurring just about every other word.

"What's the big attraction?" I enquired of his companion, who introduced himself as "John Boy" Walton, also from West Virginia.

"The smell of the octane," he replied. "I'm a Dale Earnhardt fan," he explained, recounting what for him had clearly been a life-changing experience. "I went into a barber shop years ago, and a guy was raggin' on Dale, sayin' he was a piece of garbage, not a good driver, and the barber put the guy out the door. That's when I took an interest."

Following the racing circuit sets them each back about three hundred dollars a weekend in tickets, gas and beer. But it was worth every cent. Bruce explained that Richmond was a short track, just three-quarters of a mile, so the cars would be running closer together, making tonight's race even more exhilarating. "On the straightaway, they're at a hundred and fifty miles an hour, hundred and twenty miles when they go into the corners. You can smell the exhaust," he said. During the week he and John Boy made their living in construction and had once had the privilege of laying concrete for one of the big racetracks in the South-east. They were the type of Americans who worked hard, played hard and were proud to be called rednecks. John Boy even supplied his own definition.

"Redneck is somebody who doesn't mow the yard, and who drinks a lot of beer," he said as he opened another can.

"Get 'er done!" shouted a girl nearby, who was following the progress of an impromptu game of horseshoes.

"Yeah, get 'er done!" echoed the entire group of assembled spectators. Perhaps that is the slogan of the times for red America — a quintessentially hillbilly motto embodying determination, hope and humour.

If the politicians were eyeing up this group to attract white working-class men, they had better come and see for themselves. The place quickly filled up not just with "NASCAR Dads", but also with NASCAR mothers, grandmothers and girlfriends.

"Why do you come?" I asked a woman clad in a tight top and shorts, who was moving suggestively to the sound of a Kenny Chesney song floating out from the inside of a truck.

"Honey, the attraction is . . . Look at all the men! I mean you got 'em tall, short. You got 'em with long pants, short pants. You got 'em drunk, you got 'em sober. You got a bunch of guys riding round in fast cars, right?!"

An attorney's secretary in rural Virginia, she was a hardcore motor racing fan. "I named my dog, my snake, even my son, all after Dale Earnhardt," she said, leaving me wondering if she was pulling my leg. Her take on the stereotypical rural female was short and to the point.

"She's a girl who doesn't take any shit from her man!" she laughed. "Are you wearing a bra?" she then asked, staring at my shirt.

"Yeah, it's down there somewhere," I answered, realising too late that not wearing one would have admitted me to the redneck club without further ado.

Part of the genius of George Bush is that he managed to convince these people not once, but twice, that he is just like them. Even if he did go to prep school and to Yale and was part of an established political dynasty, it doesn't matter. George Bush walks like an outdoors man and talks like a cowboy. He shoots from the hip and can connect with the ordinary Joe in ways that no Democrat could hope to do. When he taunted the insurgent enemy in Iraq by saying "Bring 'em on", he was not talking to the New York/Washington liberal axis who were so offended by that comment. He was speaking to the "Get 'er done" crowd.

HAVING DISCLOSED TO NUMEROUS NASCAR regulars that this was my first time, the consensus was that I would either love it or hate it. And if it turned out to be the former, I would be back again! There was no denying it. I was fresh from blue America, and I was sure I wasn't fooling anyone. But I did have some experience of rally driving in Ireland. Following an old boyfriend around on the Tarmac Challenge circuit, to spots like Omagh and Ballina, had been as exciting as it ever got. He was a navigator on a two-man team, and I had spent most weekends praying that they would both make it home alive. As a spectator, though, I had found the sport dull. Races were held on minor roads closed off for the occasion and allowing for only fleeting views. Blink and you'd miss your car, which might not come around again for another hour. Invariably the rain came down, soaking the fans — not to mention the odd car leaving the tarmac and cutting right through them. I had generally resorted to sitting in a car reading the newspaper and scoffing "hang sandwiches", a rudimentary form of tailgating. I had almost brought a book with me to Richmond, just in case.

"I don't even drive fast," I explained my reservations to Alisha Chiarky, as we waited for the transport from the tailgating field to the racetrack.

"Oh, I don't drive at all," she said.

"And you enjoy this?"

"The faster the better!"

Alisha was a thin woman well into her seventies, with shoulder-length grey hair, silver-rimmed glasses and a cigarette hanging from her lips as she spoke. "The smell, the excitement, it gets your adrenaline pumping. I wouldn't miss it." From a bag she produced a set of expensive-looking headphones, and a scanner which she would use to hear what the drivers were saying as they drove. If she keyed in numbers provided on the race programme, she could be right there with them as they plunged around the track.

"I want to see it all. Hear it all. What they are going to do when they go into the pit. What tyres they need. What's too loose or too taut, and how it all needs to be fixed in fourteen seconds."

The thrill-seeking grandmother took a drag from her cigarette as she savoured the experience to come. She was the umpteenth person who spoke about the smell of the fuel as though it were some magical elixir.

In the long line for the toilets, religious conversions were being sought by a small middle-aged woman, who had come all the way from Washington State on the west coast.

"Accept Jesus," she repeated, as she handed out copies of a cartoon created by her husband for NASCAR fans.

The cartoon strip told the story of a local God-fearing motor-racing hero, who saw that his chief rival, "Kid California", was a heathen and tried to get him to turn to Jesus. Alas, the "Kid" didn't pay any attention and was killed in a fiery crash without being saved. It was the same message I had heard so often in rural America — you'd better be letting the good Lord in before it's too late.

"I was raised in a church which wasn't working for me," the woman explained, confirming that Americans have been deserting mainstream religious denominations in favour of independent evangelical groups. "Now I'm getting the message out that everybody needs to receive Jesus for their personal salvation. No church or good works can do that," she believed.

In targeting NASCAR fans she was trying to mix racing with religion but no one was paying her much heed and most of the cartoon strips ended up on the ground. I wondered how difficult it must be for someone to stand there and try to attract attention for anything other than race programmes or beer. I have never relished approaching people on the street with a TV camera looking for comments. The chances of being told to get lost were always quite high. But if I wanted to gauge public opinion, I had to do it. This woman with the cartoon strips probably hated standing there too, but evangelicals are obliged to try and convert others. And she couldn't do that sitting at home.

MY CONVERSION TO NASCAR BEGAN shortly thereafter when, looking around the merchandise stands, I decided to swap my sweltering jeans for a pair of Dale Earnhardt Jr shorts. The logo on the left thigh of my shorts read "The Intimidator". This change of attire granted me some small sense of belonging. But I was still the only woman in sight who had turned up with sandals and a handbag. The uniform of a redneck American girl at play is white tennis shoes and socks and a "fanny pack" — the quaint term for a purse that you tie around your waist. Everybody also had their backpacks full of snacks and beer. One of the concessions that attracts working-class Americans to motor-racing is that, instead of paying through the nose for alcohol inside the stadium, you can bring your own. There were plenty of food stands, all catering to the deep-fried tastes of red America. You wouldn't dare to ask for a coffee or a sun-dried tomato salad around here.

Closer to the entrance, the route was lined with ostentatious camper vans, some as big as houses with pop-out rooms and generators. The tour buses were there too, the drivers' chiselled faces staring out from the sides of the huge vehicles, which doubled up as souvenir shops. It was hard to miss driver No. 6, sponsored by the makers of America's fastest-selling prescription drug, Viagra.

Entering the grandstand itself was mesmerising. The sheer size of the oval arena reduced the people in the stands to tiny coloured specks. The track glistened in the evening sun and, in the infield, satellite trucks and camera crews sat ready to bring this American Revolution to life for the millions watching at home. Then one hundred and ten thousand people stood and sang "The Star-Spangled Banner". Though I am not American, the sight and sound of so many people singing the praises of their country always sends a stray tear scuttling down my face.

A voice over the loudhailer asked for a moment's silence to remember an eighteen-year-old local female soldier who had just been killed in Iraq. The stadium was hushed. Though many of those present probably did not know anyone serving, it is from their ranks that many of the enlisted soldiers are drawn, young kids looking for a free education or the benefits that come from joining the National Guard. In a sense this has been red America's war. White working-class Americans, struggling to keep their heads above water and their values intact, have latched on to it perhaps as a way of showing strength and anger. They are angry with Democrats who they say have deserted them, angry with Republicans who they suspect may be fooling them, and above all they are angry with anyone who dares mess with America. Perhaps they saw supporting the war as a chance to feel strong again, to feel in charge. They had stuck with the President, bought his ideas about protecting America and spreading freedom. Now they were hoping they were not being let down again.

The quiet reflection on the fallen female soldier was shattered by a sonic explosion as four fighter jets appeared out of nowhere and tore over our heads in formation. I almost climbed under the seat with the fright, but it was all just part of the show. Two minutes later the eight hundred horsepower engines of the race cars let out a communal roar, as the drivers barrelled around the track at speed. Though deafening to the uninitiated ear, this was only the warm-up. By the time the actual race got going, the sound was more like a million bees buzzing at once. And yes, you could smell the octane and the burning rubber. I held my breath as the forty-three cars came around the corner almost as one, their numbers now indistinguishable, only streaks of colour visible. First yellow, then orange, or was that Earnhardt Jr in the red? BzzzzzZZZZZ. Round and round they came, lapping the track every twenty seconds. Round and round, again and again and again.

After five minutes, I was one of the few spectators left standing, my mouth still hanging open. The experienced fans had sat down to wait for the first smash-up of the night.

They say most car accidents take place in the rural parts of America and that scenes of carnage are nothing new to most people. Drivers do tend to stare at crash scene as they pass, and we all find ourselves speculating about what might or might not have happened. At a NASCAR event, you just watch it all unfold from the comfort of your bleacher, beer and hotdog in hand. In my initial state of euphoria, I had not noticed the ambulances lined up at every turn of the track, ready to charge out if necessary. It didn't take long to see them go. Fifteen minutes into the race, with the pack still sticking close together, one car hit the siding, flipped over three times and disappeared in a cloud of smoke. The entire arena stood up. The noise level dropped dramatically as the other cars prepared to stop. Now I wished I had a scanner and headphones. Alisha, my elderly friend, would know what was going on — whether or not the driver was hurt, if he had made it out of the car, and who it was that had crashed out so soon.

Minutes later a fireproofed figure walked away from the wreck and the ambulances returned to their positions. BzzzzzZZZZZZZ. They were off again. Round and round and round.

As the stadium lights took over from the fading sun, the place became that field of dreams that hooks even the most casual observer into its dizzying spell. Down by the edge of the track, the cars played tricks with my eyes. Looking as though they would certainly hit the wall, they swung around into the straightaway, then tucked in again real close, just before making the next left turn. The warm wind kicked up by their energy and motion hit against my face, and I even pulled fragments of rubber from my hair. This was getting down and dirty, and it was a lot of fun. Maybe I, too, was a redneck at heart. I come from rural Ireland and, though I've spent most of my adult life in crowded cities, they do say "You can take the girl out of the country, but you can't take the country out of the girl!"

AND SO IT CONTINUED FOR FOUR HUNDRED LAPS and five crashes. Number 9, Kasey Khane, a twenty-five-year-old racer, registered his first big career win and drenched his face in champagne to celebrate. His prize for risking his life in front of all of us was half a million dollars. Far from its dirt track days back in the Old South, American motor racing has entered its golden era. Television deals and merchandise sales alone are reportedly worth five billion dollars a year. Long-time fans argue that the sport of rednecks is selling out to commercialism, and are horrified by talk that it may soon be opened up to Toyotas! This could be the last hurrah for the simple pleasure derived from watching American-made cars competing with one another. The way things are going, American car manufacturers could eventually be taken over by the Japanese. Companies like Ford are no longer willing to pay the wages and health benefits American workers need to survive. Companies are being asked to pay five dollars an hour per employee just to cover health insurance.

The NASCAR crowd didn't seem to want to get into lengthy discussions about politics with a European journalist. They know what Europe thinks and their attitude is that Europe does not wish America well. Blue America, they believe, is not much better than Europe. They share similar worldviews and similar liberal values. If the reds don't stand up for America, they fear nobody will.

In the meantime, the two nations exist side by side but separately. They even get their news from different sources. Red America watches the Fox channel and listens to conservative talk show hosts Rush Limbaugh and Sean Hannity. Blue America reads the *New York Times* and listens to National Public Radio. Red America goes hunting and fishing, and shops at Wal-Mart. Blue America goes to the movies and Macy's. Of course, these are all dangerous generalisations. But they have stuck and contribute even further to each side's fear of the other. The "NASCAR Dads" didn't seem to be aware that they will be a major target for both parties in the 2008 election. They have switched allegiances before and, if the Republicans keep losing jobs and troops, they could potentially switch again.

Leaving the track at midnight, most fans were headed back to their accommodation in tailgate city, to down a few more beers and look forward to the next day of racing. Bruce and John Boy from West Virginia were spending the night in their truck and would tackle the traffic in the morning. Despite the quantity of alcohol consumed, nobody seemed obviously inebriated or out of control. But then light beer is the official drink of red America.

For days afterwards I had the smell of the octane in my nostrils and the feel of the hot wind on my face each time I saw a car breaking the speed limit. For a while I thought nothing of being stuck in traffic on the highway. I have not gone back to the track since, but every now and then I tune in to a race on the television for news of Dale Earnhardt Jr. After all, I have a pair of shorts named after him.

Chapter 6

The Pope on the Prairie

I THOUGHT I HAD SEEN out-of-the-way, middle-of-nowhere America, until I came to Kansas. This is the rectangular state at the very heart of the country, the centre point between the east and west coasts. Leaving Kansas City, which straddles the border with Missouri, I drove eighty miles west to Topeka, a dreary city surrounded by smoking industrial chimneys. I then veered thirty miles north, driving through continuously flat yellow crop country. You could go for miles around and not see another car, which, for me, was a good thing. I was still getting used to driving on American roads. For four years as a television correspondent I had ridden with my cameraman, Harvey, who could see that driving was not one of my talents and strongly advised me against it. But you can't get far in rural America without a car, so I had to start. Eventually I turned off onto a smaller road, which had the look of a country lane that might dead-end in a field somewhere. But after ten minutes of bouncing along on gravel, kicking up clouds of dust as I went, I came to the town of Delia, Kansas.

Delia is more of an encampment than a town. It is comprised of about fifty homes that have the appearance of being half mobile and half rooted to the ground — as though they might suddenly take flight, like the house in the classic Kansas story *The Wizard of Oz*. The spaces around the homes are littered with disused cars, children's toys and bits of old farm machinery, yet the owners are proud enough to advertise their names on wooden plaques and stone carvings by the front doors. At ten in the morning, the only sound to be heard in the town was the blowing of the wind, punctuated every now and then by a Union Pacific freight train trundling by with a load of timber. Commercial Delia appeared to be confined to a tiny post office, its sole employee loitering by the door, dragging on a mid-morning cigarette. Across the road, an establishment now long disestablished bore the name "Matyak Garage". Its mottled walls and broken windows screamed "tear me down or fix me up", but no one had bothered to do either and the heap of rotting real estate just sat there weeping.

David Bawden keeps a low profile, living about two miles outside of Delia off the end of an isolated lane. He did create a bit of a stir ten years earlier when he declared himself Pope, but these days nobody bothers him much, and that's the way he likes it. He had displayed a touch of the Great Oz when I had e-mailed him through his website, www.vaticaninexile.com, twice in one day requesting an audience.

"The papal secretary only checks e-mail once a week. Please be patient," came the reply. Well, my guess is, the papal secretary answered the door to me when I arrived at the light blue wooden house.

"Welcome, I'm Mrs Bawden, the Pope's mother," she greeted me.

Dressed in a royal blue smock, flip flops and large red-rimmed glasses, Clara Bawden was positively beaming as she led me inside to her well-kept living room. To the front was a simple dining section and at the rear a more comfortable lounging area. Back there, seated in a brightly lit corner, was her eldest son dressed in a long white cassock and a papal cap. He was much younger than I had expected, much too young to be pope. Unlike so many people you meet in middle America, he was a fit and trim forty-six-year-old. For a fleeting moment, I wondered if they expected me to kneel and kiss the ring that I spotted on his right hand, but I avoided any fake adulation, opting for a firm handshake, before they proceeded to tell me how this all came about.

Clara had moved from Texas to Oklahoma as a young woman, after hearing about the Society of St Pius X, a traditionalist Roman Catholic group. She had been an old-school Roman Catholic upset by the doctrinal changes introduced in the 1960s by Vatican II and particularly by the loss of the Latin Mass. Around 1970, controversial Archbishop Marcel Lefebvre had set up the Society of St Pius X in Switzerland for the purpose of retaining the old ways. He and his followers believed that priests should continue to face the altar during mass, keeping their backs to the congregation. They wanted women to keep their heads covered in church and felt that hugs and handshakes, such as exchanging the sign of peace, were modernist nonsense. Archbishop Lefebvre was tolerated by the Vatican, until he began ordaining his own bishops, when he was declared to be in schism with the church. But his society continued to profess loyalty to the Pope in Rome, and today it claims to have tens of thousands of followers around the world, including about twenty thousand in the US.

David Bawden had attended the Society's school in St Mary's, a small town about fifteen miles from Delia. But the Bawdens fell out with the Society after David's plans for ordination as a priest ran into trouble. He says he spent a year at their seminary in Econe, Switzerland, before being dismissed without explanation. Refused readmission, the Bawdens decided to take matters into their own hands. They would skip the priesthood and go straight for the papacy.

"Sedevacantism" was the key to him becoming Pope, David explained, as he shifted in his armchair, his hands joined and resting on his chest. This belief claims that the Pope in Rome is technically a heretic and that the papal throne is therefore vacant. David and his mother had concluded that successive popes had abandoned Christ's original doctrine by relaxing rules on fasting and self-discipline, and by cavorting at the Vatican with Jews and Hindus, whom they regarded as enemies of the "one true church". David Bawden had written a book about this, then he had called a papal election, which he had held at a thrift store owned by his late father near the town of Delia. A total of six people had shown up: David, his parents and a few family friends. Unanimously installed as pontiff, he took the name Michael. Pope Michael claims to have about a hundred committed followers around the world, and told me he gets scores of hits on his website every day.

Despite managing to look and sound remarkably like a man of the cloth, Bawden admitted that he was not taken seriously in Kansas. "No, but I didn't expect to be. Local people are friendly, that's all," he said.

After the election, *The Kansas City Star* had called the Vatican in Rome for a comment but none had been forthcoming and things had been quiet since then. "This is the age of indifference," his mother weighed in. "You can be whomever you want to be and people just say 'right on'." The St Pius X Society was paying no attention to "his holiness" either, not since he had badmouthed it in a series of articles in the local newspaper.

"They don't take my claim to the papacy at all seriously."

"And does that bother you?"

"I'm not here to be liked, but to do the work of Christ."

Delusional would be the most tempting conclusion when faced with Pope Michael of Kansas and his mother, but this papal double act had all the answers. For over two decades they had studied church doctrine, mainly from books picked up at second-hand stores and garage sales. Clara's eyes lit up as she enquired if I was familiar with garage sales — her favourite pastime. I had indeed browsed through the assorted junk that Americans set out on their front lawns after spring cleaning, on the off-chance that somebody might want to buy it. It was always the type of stuff they should be paying you to take away: candlesticks, old photographs of strangers, decades-old copies of *Time* and *Life* magazines and outdated academic volumes harvested from dusty basements. "We couldn't afford all these books if we had to buy them new," she pointed to the bulging shelves in the Pope's study.

As I tried to walk them through the logic behind their claim to the papacy, mother and son argued loudly over church history, the works of the saints and the gospels. Technically, for all anyone knows, the Bawdens could be correct and, leaving aside their refusal to consider the challenges facing the modern church and their devotion to religious conspiracy theories, I still had to admire their dogged determination to save the faith in what they saw as its purest form. From what I could tell, money didn't seem to be a motivating factor. They had no scams going and they weren't selling anything. They claimed to be living comfortably out of savings and family inheritances.

"And what of my Roman Catholic faith?" I enquired of the Pope of Kansas.

"You have been deceived, you and millions of other Roman Catholics; deceived by those in the Church who have abandoned the faith," he informed me. Pope Paul VI, he reckoned from his own studies and observations, had apparently been among the worst offenders in this regard, stooping so low as to wear a Jewish *ephod* — a high priest's outfit — in the Vatican. He also had a theory that Paul VI was the antichrist referred to in the Book of Revelations. Reaching for a book, he produced a copy of that pontiff's signature and, turning it upside down, demonstrated how it looked just like three sixes.

It was time to bring up the subject of a rival pope I'd caught wind of in Montana, but it turned out there are half a dozen other claimants to the papacy. "Pope Gregory XVII in Spain just died," he revealed, with no hint of regret, "and there's a Gregory XIX, back east somewhere, I just had an e-mail from him the other day."

The Montana pontiff, Clara interrupted, was not legally elected because he had held a phone-in vote.

"You can't elect a pope by a vote over the phone," she insisted; "you have to be physically present." Pope Michael's conclave, back in 1996, had accepted votes only from those present on the day.

Because of their rejection of the new mass or *novus ordo*, the Bawdens were not attending services anywhere or receiving the sacraments. Pope Michael argued that, because of the Vatican II changes, it was possible there were now no real masses being said anywhere in the world, except by a few bishops in Russia who had yet to surface because of continuing religious oppression there. What America's sixty million Catholics were being offered, he believed, was not a true celebration of the Eucharist.

"We just pray here now," Clara explained, offering me a lace veil as we went upstairs and entered a little chapel in the attic. The triangular space had an ecclesiastical ambiance. The attic's wooden beams were covered with white sheets and a simple table served as an altar. On it was an ornate golden piece, a sort of tabernacle. The kneelers were home-made. The three of us bowed our heads and were quiet for several moments. Kneeling beside a forty-six-year-old unemployed man in a white cassock, I had to admit to myself that I wasn't sure which of us was most in need of divine help — him, or me for being there.

At lunch downstairs, Pope Michael blessed our salami and cheese by making the sign of the cross with two fingers joined, just as any pope would. As we ate, he abandoned the pontificating and chatted amiably about a range of issues. He was deeply worried about the American economy. His brother, an electrician with six children, often had to go over the border to Nebraska and even up to Canada for work. There was a nun in the family too, he disclosed — a legitimately ordained Sister of Charity — over in

Leavenworth, near Kansas City. "We don't talk religion when she comes," Clara volunteered, warning me away from any further probing on that subject.

Before I left, they evaluated the current state of the Roman Catholic Church which was, they feared, still in decline. "The church reached its peak back in the thirteenth century," Clara said, adding that it had been mainly downhill from there. That was the period just before the papacy left Rome and was based for several decades in the French town of Avignon. We all agreed that any hope of it being based in Kansas in the near future was slim-to-nothing, though Pope Michael assured me that he would continue to get his message out using the internet, and maybe by taking a trip next door to Colorado, where apparently he had a decent following. I wondered if he would ever think of moving to New York where he might attract more attention.

"No," he said firmly. "If I move anywhere, it will be to Rome, my home diocese."

I nodded gravely and thanked him and his mother for their hospitality. After a photograph on the front porch, I left them in their Vatican-in-exile and drove away, back through the dust and the north Kansas prairie.

SIXTY MILES OR SO SOUTH of Delia, I came to the old pioneer town of Council Grove, population two thousand three hundred. Kansas has just thirty-two people per square mile, as opposed to the fifty thousand who crowd into that same space in Manhattan. One hundred and fifty years ago, Council Grove was the last stop for rest and supplies for traders setting out on the Santa Fe Trail. Beyond it was just wilderness. At the entrance to the town, the stump of an oak tree marks the spot where in 1825 a treaty was signed with the Kanza Indian tribe allowing safe passage through native lands for the white man. The "Council Oak", as it was called, blew down in a storm some years back but the stump is still there.

Council Grove is now ninety-six per cent white, less than one per cent Native American.

The town looks a bit more permanent than it did back in the old trail days, when photos show it as a collection of makeshift cabins. There is one wide street that runs for seven or eight blocks, with low-slung buildings that evoke something of the old West, and cars and trucks still pull in here with their headlights facing the kerb, the way horses and wagons used to. Like all small American towns I've been through, it seems to be in the middle of a long commercial slumber. The main street is home to chiropractors, thrift stores and insurance agents — hardly the type of attractions that bring the masses into town.

Inside an old bank building I met Ken McClintock and stepped back fifty years. An attorney, McClintock was carrying out his business from behind the iron grille where the bank teller once sat.

"About that minor in possession of alcohol, we want to go for a plea bargain."

I heard his voice before I spotted him crouched behind the fat files piled on his desk. His bargain struck, he opened up a side door and led me to the inner sanctum. Ken was a diminutive man of about sixty-five, dressed in a pink shirt and brown business suit. He had a full beard and small round glasses. As well as being a man of the law, he is also the local historian. A brief description of life in Council Grove confirmed that, while keeping its head above water, the town was struggling. Locals had worked hard to preserve its biggest asset — its past — but there was just one small hotel in town for tourists, and a new visitors' centre for the Tall Grass Prairie Reserve, about ten miles away, had not been as big a draw as expected. There were still the odd European visitors like me tripping through and a few Japanese tourists obsessed with the American Wild West.

I didn't need to ask if I was in Bush country. Every county in Kansas except two had voted for the President. "People here are politically conservative," Ken said, explaining that they were attracted by the low taxes and smaller government ideas of the Republicans. Following the libertarian model of social justice, modern Republican thinking preaches self-reliance over welfare. If people need to be rescued, they should look to charities. It's hard to see how this appeals to the poor, who might well need the odd handout to survive when manufacturers close their doors and move off to China or when a tornado carries their house away. But the attitude in rural America is different from that in the cities.

"We don't like having people back in Washington telling us how to do every little thing," Ken explained, suggesting that the less regulation and control coming from the centre, the better. The Republican's outright dedication to big business bothered him, it even maddened him, but he would put up with it rather than switch to the Democrats, who, he felt, were on the wrong side of too many social issues.

"So moral issues are important to people here?"

"Sure, you are all the time hearing about the crazy things they are doing out in California and to some extent on the east coast too. The interest groups that pop up for different causes undermine how we thought this country should have been run all along. In California, they even want to take religion out of the boy scouts' organisation. They are not content with getting religion out of schools; they have to get it out of every aspect of life."

That morning as I had pulled into Council Grove, moral and ethical issues were top of the news yet again. A Florida woman named Terri Schiavo had died two weeks after the courts ordered that the feeding tube keeping her alive be removed. After collapsing and suffering cardiac arrest, the forty-one-year-old had been in a vegetative state for fifteen years, but her family was split over whether or not she should be kept alive. Schiavo's estranged husband wanted her to be allowed to die and the courts had backed him, but as she slowly dehydrated without food or water, her distraught parents pleaded for help to have the decision reversed. President Bush jumped straight in, signing emergency legislation to have the tube reinserted. But the courts ignored this too, and for two weeks America ranted and raved as the woman slowly slipped away. The Roman Catholic Church sided with the President, right-to-die groups sided with the husband, and cable television supplied the pathos, constantly replaying footage of Schiavo, first as an attractive young woman before her illness and then as a patient lying helpless in a hospital bed, her blinking eyes the only sign that she was alive.

Ken McClintock, I assumed, would have backed the President on this too, but as it turned out he had his own story to tell. His mother had passed away quietly in a nursing home without food, after the family had decided not to insert a feeding tube to keep her alive. "She didn't know anybody around her or what was going on," he reflected, telling me that she had succumbed to Alzheimer's a decade earlier. When, eventually, she was unable to swallow her food, the family had decided to let her go. "We could have kept her around several more years but the only benefit would have been to the nursing home," he said, adding that his elderly father would have been bankrupted by now. Instead, he had been able to give his money towards the building of a new church in the town.

The McClintocks were pretty practical when it came to religion too. Ken and his wife Shirley had switched churches a few times. They belonged to the mainstream Protestant family but shopping around for a new denomination was not at all unusual. Whether you were a Methodist, a Presbyterian or an Episcopalian, he stressed, very much depended on your liking for the pastor and whether or not the church was convenient. I had been encountering this consumer choice aspect of religion right across America. Families and individuals were treating religious denominations just like any other commodity.

Take the Bushes. George H.W. Bush, the forty-first president, and his wife Barbara are Presbyterians, but their son George W. had joined the United Methodist Church, while his brother Jeb, the Governor of Florida, had left the Protestant family altogether to become a Roman Catholic after he had married a Mexican. In this new era of choice, everyone in the family could attend separate churches on a Sunday, and then all meet up back home for dinner, without any arguments or tensions.

Since it was getting close to lunchtime, I asked Ken if he could recommend something that did not involve fries or a large Diet Coke. "Oh, my wife runs a little bakery café right up the street," he said.

"I'll give it a try," I said, and left him to get back to his files and his plea bargains.

THE OLD TERWILLIGER HOME, where the café was located, was the last house that pioneers passed before hitting the Santa Fe Trail. Everything in Council Grove was "last chance". The last chance store at the top of the town looked as if it had not been touched since it closed its doors over a century earlier. A tourist sign outside indicated that in its heyday it was last chance for "bacon, beans and whiskey". By the time I had found the McClintock's "last chance for a decent lunch" establishment, Ken was already there waiting tables. He had managed to do a very quick costume change, replacing his lawyer's attire with a black waistcoat and a grandfather shirt. His wife was how I imagine Laura Ingalls from the television show *Little House on the Prairie* might have looked as a grandmother. Shirley McClintock wore a long skirt and high-necked blouse fixed tightly at the throat with a brooch. She wore her hair in braids and had rimless round glasses.

"Can I help you?"

"I'd like to eat. I was just with your husband downtown," I pointed back into the kitchen where Ken had disappeared with a tray of dishes.

"Would you like to try our buffalo sandwich?"

I had never eaten buffalo and assumed the animal to be so rare as to end up as a tourist attraction, not a sandwich, but I decided to give it a go. There was just one other person left in the café and he turned out to be Ken's father, whom we had spoken about earlier. Taking a break from his soup, the old man nodded in my direction.

"How are you today, sir?" I gave the traditional greeting.

No answer.

"He's very deaf," Shirley told me, before yelling at the old man: "She's from IRE-LAND."

"Oh, she's a foreigner," he replied and returned to his soup.

My buffalo sandwich arrived, accompanied by a serving of barbecued beans. It was delicious. The meat was sweet and tender and just slightly gamey, even though it had not been slaughtered in the wild. "Kill it and grill it" is still one of rural America's enduring obsessions, but the buffalo on my plate, I had to assume, had not been shot by Ken McClintock, lawyer, historian and waiter.

Shirley, a retired schoolteacher, provided me with a potted history of American morality from the roaring 1920s through the more lean and conservative times of the Great Depression and World War II and on to the 1960s, when she felt the real damage had been done. The rise of atheism, the Vietnam War, and the drugs scene, she felt, had all contributed to America's downfall. Though things were still in a pitiful state, she suspected that the children of the baby boomers were turning conservative again — ironically, as a rebellion against their hedonistic 1960s-era parents.

I had heard this argument before, back in Maryland, from the parents of a young soldier serving in Iraq. Both mother and father were dyed-in-the-wool Democrats who had protested against the Vietnam War. Now, over thirty years later, they found themselves in the position of having to raise money to buy proper body-armour for their son who was fighting insurgents. After the invasion of Iraq in 2003, the military had run short of armour and platoon members were tossing coins each morning to determine who would get to wear the protective gear for the day.

"How did your twenty-year-old son end up in this situation if you are so against war?" I had asked when I met them at their home on Maryland's eastern shore.

"Oh, these days, the most effective way for kids to rebel against their liberal parents is to join the army or the Republican Party," the soldier's mother had explained as I sat watching her pack bug spray, a telephone card and snacks into a cardboard box bound for the Iraqi desert. She couldn't tell me exactly where her son was serving. If anyone knew that kind of information, she said, he would probably be killed.

KEN MCCLINTOCK GRABBED HIS BRIEFCASE and, tossing on his hat and overcoat, bolted for the door. "I've got a court appearance at one o'clock," he shouted over his shoulder. I planned to follow him, to see justice, Council Grove style, but within minutes he was back again with the news that his case had been settled.

Before leaving the next day, I called in to Shirley McClintock at the café to say goodbye. I wished her and Council Grove well, knowing how badly she and Ken wanted the place to thrive. The town would be fine, she reckoned, if the drugs didn't destroy it.

"Drugs?" I asked.

"Oh yes, and not just the kids but the adults too," she added, revealing the darker side of life in small-town America. "It's those damn meth labs," she sighed.

Makeshift laboratories making the highly addictive "crystal meth" were springing up like dandelions. Using ingredients available over the counter in every pharmacy in the country, the concoction, also known as "ice" or "glass", was being heavily produced in Kansas and in the neighbouring states of Missouri and Iowa. It was becoming the drug of choice at parties, while truck drivers were among the biggest customers, using it to stay awake on their cross-country journeys. Shirley, the prudent motherly type, filled me in on its aphrodisiac effects. "It makes sex feel like you've never had it before," she told me, adding quickly that Ken was working with a local group to try to stop the scourge.

All this was percolating through my head as I drove out of Council Grove in the April sunshine. I had imagined it as a typical rural Republican town, but found that this was only half the picture. The locals held on to dreams of economic prosperity yet the small businesses were being squeezed out by corporate America. They yearned to reverse moral decline, yet drug abuse was rampant. Small-town values were what they wanted, but boredom and utter dissatisfaction with life were in danger of dragging the place down to the level of an inner-city ghetto. Council Grove was a story of competing forces in action. Call it past versus present, good versus evil, or red versus blue — whatever the labels, a monumental struggle is underway. Since leaving Washington months earlier, this was as close as I had come to understanding what twenty-first century America is about.

I TOOK ROUTE 177 SOUTH and stopped at the Tall Grass Prairie Reserve which the McClintocks had recommended. The information booth was deserted, so I showed myself around. The unique ecosystem of tall reed-like grass had once covered most of the American Midwest, but modern farming had consigned much of it to the plough and only this last area remained intact. They say the soil here is so rich they still bring cattle all the way up from Texas to graze. Farther on, I pulled into a cemetery, which revealed that the Irish had been through Kansas. The names Maloney, Clarke and Boylan had been carved into headstones as far back as 1860. They must have come from Cork on the coffin ships and headed out west with the pioneers and wagon trains. Whatever their story, the scene could not have been much different then than it is now. Out on the prairie there is still no sound except the birds singing and the wind blowing through the grass.

Back in 2003 I had witnessed a new generation of Irish explorers checking out the American prairie in South Dakota, two states north of Kansas. There is a shortage of dairy farmers there and someone thought the Irish, with their history of hardship and perseverance, might be the boys to take up the slack. They had invited anyone who might be interested in making the move to come and spend a week looking around. These Irishmen and women didn't travel in open wagons, as their nineteenth-century predecessors had. They came in heated tour buses and were armed with digital cameras. For a week they were ferried to towns smaller than Council Grove and farms bigger than most Irish parishes. In most of America, small farms are a thing of the past. Old MacDonald has long since sold out to his neighbour and his neighbour's neighbour to form the large enterprises needed to service the agribusiness giants. Farmers with one hundred head of cattle back home were being shown around operations where over a thousand animals were being milked around the clock. The wide open spaces and freezing winter were far too bleak for these potential migrants. They went home, probably never intending to set foot back in South Dakota, and unable to believe their bad luck that RTÉ had been there to record the whole episode!

My journey out of Kansas coincided with the final hours of Pope John Paul II's life. As I drove, one radio station reported prematurely that he had died. Everyone on the airwaves agreed that he had been a major figure of the twentieth century. Some commentators compared him incongruously to Ronald Reagan and credited the two men with bringing an end to the Cold War.

I pulled in to a truck-stop for lunch, the sort that caters for the big eighteen-wheelers. The first time I had driven alone in the US, I had cowered in the right-hand lane, astounded by the sheer size of these rigs. If you happen to find yourself behind one, in front of one and beside one all at once, with their huge engines screaming, you just hold your breath. Passing one of them is like overtaking a train. This was a full-service truck-stop with showers and gambling machines and the ubiquitous all-you-can-eat buffet. I thought people might be following the news of the Pope but the drivers were all busy freshening up and phoning home.

"Driver No. 3 to shower No. 1," a voice came over the public address system. I did a double take as a blonde woman of hefty proportions, dressed all in baby pink and carrying a purple vanity case, headed for the showers. Trucker Barbie: surely someone would be able to patent her. There was also a trucker's chapel in an outhouse near the petrol pumps. It was locked but a note on the door invited drivers to Sunday worship. By the pay-phones, I found free copies of the New Testament and taped readings from the Bible. If you weren't using "crystal meth" to keep on truckin', there was always the Jesus alternative.

"BREAKING NEWS: THE POPE is near death tonight at the Vatican." Later that afternoon, the CNN announcer's voice interrupted the noise and general chaos of the Kansas City airport lounge where I was waiting for a flight out.

"He's been near death for months," I heard a father say to his two young boys who agreed that it wasn't really breaking news then. During my flight the Pope did pass away. I thought of David Bawden, alias Pope Michael, sitting in Delia with his mother and wondered if they might be planning to travel to Rome to take advantage of this hiatus.

The plane shook violently as we descended into Baltimore Airport. I hate flying and I was starting to shiver. Beside me a young mother tried to calm her baby girl who was screeching, more from boredom than fear. When I feel the plane is about to crash, which is on almost every flight, I have to talk to someone. I turned to the mother just as the jet swerved sharply downwards and to the right, causing others to gasp aloud.

"Are you not scared?" I asked her.

She looked at me and smiled sweetly.

"No, I know the Lord will take care of me."

There it was again. American faith.

And I still had not got the hang of it.

Chapter 7

Holy Guacamole

COMING FROM IRELAND, I have yet to get used to the fact that most of rural America's eating spots are found not on quaint little streets in the centre of town but in strip malls and parking lots along the highway. At the end of any exit off a main road, you can enjoy ethnic food from places as diverse as Italy and Vietnam. You'll notice that these restaurants don't have any windows, so you can pretend to be in Tuscany as you sip your Chianti and savour your perfectly cooked pasta to the sound of opera music being piped through the dimly lit room. Looking out a window at four lanes of speeding traffic would just ruin the ambiance.

Off Route 50 in Maryland, I pulled in to one of these windowless wonders, a low brick building with plastic cacti coming out of the roof. Its name, "On the Border", evoked daring escapades across the dividing line between Mexico and the United States. Like the fake Irish pubs that hang bodhrans and old beat-up black bicycles on the walls to remind the ex-pat of places like Manorhamilton, this place had ancient pots and pans, indigenous costumes and sunny mariachi music — a complete Mexican fantasy to accompany margaritas and burritos on a grey Maryland Saturday.

Victor the waiter was the real thing though. Like millions of Mexicans, he had embraced the harsh east-coast American winters for the chance to make money and support his family back home.

"I'm from Chiapas province," he told me, his face brightening when I told him that I intended to travel to Mexico. Victor was familiar with San Cristobal de las Casas, where I was planning to stay, and at the mention of it he became almost as excited as I was.

"Palenque, you must go to see the Mayan ruins there, the best in the whole country," he enthused. He jotted down names and suggestions on his order book, tearing out the page for me.

Victor had been at this far-flung Mexican outpost for two years now, hoping that every shift of waiting tables moved him a little closer to his dream. "I'm single, so I'll work for a while then go home and maybe set up my own business," he said optimistically. I didn't know if he was in the US legally and I didn't ask. If Victor was breaking the law, he was just one of millions.

MARYLAND IS A LONG WAY FROM MEXICO but much of the southern US was once under Spanish or Mexican rule. As late as 1836 the territory that is now Texas and known as Tejas was claimed by the newly independent Mexico. But the Tejanos revolted, bringing Mexican General Santa Anna rushing to the Alamo. He was victorious there but went on to lose the next big battle and in 1836 the territory of Texas became a republic. America's plan to absorb the new republic led to the Mexican-American War. Again Mexico lost and signed the Treaty of Guadeloupe Hidalgo, giving land to the United States which became Texas and California, as well as parts of Colorado, Utah and Nevada — a bargain at fifteen million dollars.

One hundred and fifty years later, large swathes of the southern United States appear to have fallen back to the Mexicans, not by military aggression but through migration. Across southern

Texas road signs and billboards are in Spanish as well as English and in much of southern California and in Miami, Spanish is the dominant language. Back in Maryland, a language teacher told me she no longer believed American schools should be offering Spanish as a foreign language. Given that it is so widely spoken across the US, she felt that it should be now considered an American tongue. Along the border, the two cultures meld into one. "Spanglish" a fusion of both languages, is often used to communicate and Tex-Mex food is almost as commonplace as burgers and fries. This "Mexicanisation" of the south is hardly surprising given that the rich US shares a two-thousand-mile border with a third world country. Though figures are hard to come by, the best guess is that Mexicans and other Latin Americans cross the border at a rate of one million per year. Some stay for a while just to make some money to take back, but about seven thousand Mexicans settle in the US every week.

I had earlier witnessed this modern Mexican invasion up close from Douglas, Arizona, a small border town thrown together like the set of a spaghetti western. Flat-roofed buildings line the wide streets. Old store fronts display outdated merchandise, including women's dresses and hats long gone from the fashion pages. The odd sports bar still masquerades as an old-time saloon and a hotel on the main street, the Gadsden, stands just as it did in the days of the Wild West. Fifty dollars a room doesn't guarantee much comfort these days but the Gadsden is worth the hard beds and linoleum floors. A grand wooden staircase sweeps down to a lobby where at night you can still visualise the poker games taking place and clouds of cigar smoke. Under the high ceilings and rotating fans you can almost hear the cowboys knocking back their liquor before swaggering out the saloon door and riding off into the sunset.

Douglas is hot and sweaty and in the afternoon becomes a siesta town with most people staying indoors to beat the heat. Along the southern end of town a tall wire fence separates the United States from Mexico. The reinforced mesh runs right the length of

Douglas and tapers off somewhere out in the wilderness where most of the illegal entry takes place. Looking through this fence is like peering even further back in time. The cars that cruise right up against the divide are decades-old — boat-shaped Cadillacs and Pontiacs with fins that were popular in the US forty years ago still run behind there. The Mexican houses are painted in bright pinks and oranges and appear almost luminous in the sun. Graffiti is everywhere. Over there it's still the 1960s; on the American side, it's more like the 1980s.

Most of the border-hopping takes place after dark, so a local patrol agent volunteered to take RTÉ's cameraman Harvey Cofske and me out with him on his rounds. In the early evening we drove to different points along the fence and stopped at secluded spots to watch. Only a fool would try to clear this barrier in broad daylight but by night some brave souls had cut holes in the wire with chainsaws and walked right through. We moved farther into the Arizona desert to an area unprotected by the fence, but much less hospitable to human traffic. Here the ground is rough and bone-dry and the heat unbearable by day. Unless migrants know where they are going and have sufficient water to get them there, this place is a death trap. Thousands of Mexicans are known to have died trying to cross into the US in recent years, succumbing to hypothermia in winter and heat stress and dehydration in the summer.

"They come with smuggling rings, most of them," the agent explained as we hunkered down in his truck hoping to capture some illicit movements on camera. Poor Mexicans, he said, were paying up to one thousand dollars each to smugglers to guide them across the border and into a waiting car or minibus to take them to some other part of the country. If it goes awry, they lose the money and have to start saving all over again. Some go on solo runs without any guides. "Our job is to catch them and send them back home," he stated simply.

A short time later we came across another border patrol van parked along a dirt road with two handcuffed men sitting by the back of it. They appeared to be in their twenties or thirties, ragged, sweaty, exhausted and probably very hungry. The two men stared down at their boots, avoiding making eye contact with their captors as they were questioned in Spanish. After twenty minutes it was established, just barely, that they were on their way north to find work, probably as fruit pickers. Their plan was vague but this ignominious meeting with the law barely five miles into the US seemed to be the end of it. They were loaded into the van and driven back towards Mexico.

Coming to the US illegally has always been an attractive option for the poor. In the 1980s the Irish came in droves and some of them are still living in New York and Boston without proper legal status. Now the biggest immigrant groups are Asian and Hispanic and estimates of the total number of black market workers in the US range from ten to twenty million. Nearly all of them can still find work. American farmers need labourers, the meat industry needs packers and the service industry needs workers. A cursory survey in any city around midday will reveal that most Americans are served their lunch by immigrants who later switch uniforms to go and clean up after them when they leave their offices at night. If these people were to disappear, parts of American life would just stop.

On the other side of the coin, Mexico is enormously dependent on "Western Union" money — the remittances wired back home by those who find work in the US. This income is thought to account for one-third of the Mexican economy. Both governments are fully aware of this symbiotic relationship and Mexico is forever lobbying Washington to provide an amnesty or temporary work visas to its citizens. Mexican clout is growing steadily inside the US. Hispanics, now numbering almost forty million, are a powerful force at election time and, while traditionally they have voted Democrat, they are always ready to switch sides. When they need drivers' licences and workers' permits for their illegal brothers and sisters, they are prepared to vote for whomever is singing their tune. These days they are electing their own people to office and

Hispanics have secured political positions all the way up to the White House. In 2004 George Bush offered greetings in Spanish at several campaign rallies and appointed Alberto Gonzalez as Attorney General, while in Florida his brother, Governor Jeb Bush, is married to a native Mexican.

Since September 11th, getting into America has become more difficult. Politicians on Capitol Hill are paranoid about the dangers of open borders and fear that aliens living in the shadows could potentially be plotting the next terrorist attack. Several of the hijackers who flew the planes into the Twin Towers and the Pentagon had been living locally and trained for their mission at flight schools, a fact that sent chills up the spines of every citizen. Frustrated by the lack of protection on the southern border, some Americans have started their own civilian border patrol. Calling themselves "Minutemen", probably after the elite ever-ready militia of the eighteenth-century Revolutionary War, they take up positions along the divide with Mexico, often sitting in their trucks and watching for days at a time. Armed with little more than binoculars and cell phones, they act as spotters for the police. Other objectors have not been so restrained and in some cases have shot at the Mexicans coming across. But as long as there is the promise of American jobs that pay even five dollars an hour, poverty-stricken migrants from Mexico and farther south will always take the risk.

Globalisation has also sent a considerable number of American jobs in the opposite direction to Mexico. The NAFTA (North American Free Trade Agreement) signed by President Clinton, went into effect in January 1994 and resulted early on in hundreds of American firms hopping across the border to Mexico. A day-trip to Nogales, a bustling town that straddles the line between Arizona and Mexico, revealed factory after factory lined up against the border availing of the cheap labour. Nike was there and General Motors and a range of well-known brands. The plants and warehouses looked shiny and new but the living conditions were atrocious. Workers flocking north for the jobs had set up temporary homes in what looked like refugee camps on the sides of dusty hills. Most were in shelters cobbled together with plywood and cardboard. Inside one of these a young woman was trying to raise a family while her husband worked in one of the American factories below. The two-roomed hovel was unbearably hot and fresh water could be got only from a truck which lumbered up the hill twice a day, spilling half its precious load along the way. Mexicans benefiting from NAFTA were earning a better wage than they could ever hope for in their own home towns but to get it they had to endure third-world living conditions as bad as any in Africa. Many of the factories have since moved on to other countries like Vietnam and China where the labour is even cheaper.

In the summer illegal immigrants cross into America at night when it's coolest, yet in the well-patrolled areas they have more to fear from the darkness. That's when it's easiest to get caught — thanks to infra-red technology which picks them off like a kid in a video arcade. On a bank of screens in the monitoring room at the Douglas patrol station we watched the whole sitting-duck story unfold. As soon as night falls, the immigrants, detected by the heat of their own bodies, show up as small red dots moving in groups. A patrol agent identifies their location, radios it forward to the agents in the field and the Mexicans are rounded up like a herd of goats.

"Even with all this, thousands make it by us every week," our agent admitted as we pulled over in the sagebrush to wait for a radio alert. A handsome man of about thirty, he is married to a Mexican woman. Despite serving as a roadblock to the hopes and aspirations of thousands of her fellow countrymen, he told us he loves his job.

His radio crackled into action and without a word he tore off down a dirt road at speed. As we drove, the sound of loud motors was audible ahead, like motorbikes tearing through the fields. As we got closer, we could see the lights of the small tractor-like all-terrain vehicles being used to negotiate the rough desert vegetation. By the time we reached the scene, patrol agents had caught up with about a dozen pitiful figures, nabbed as they had forged their way through the darkness to what they hoped would be a new life. They sat on the ground in a huddled group looking up into our headlights like startled deer: men and women with long black manes of hair and shabby children as young as twelve or thirteen. They looked more indigenous than many of the Mexicans I'd seen in the big cities of the North-east, and a lot more frightened. All were reluctant to talk, answering their inquisitors only in monosyllables or not at all. They wouldn't say where they were coming from or where they'd been headed. Some hid their faces — perhaps in shame or just to avoid the cameras. Others just sat in the long grass staring northwards into the black night, their sweet American dream in tatters, at least for now.

HOW EASY I HAVE IT, I thought as my United Airlines flight headed in the opposite direction, across the border into Mexico. Not so fast. There was an almighty jerking of the plane and a high-pitched scream from someone in the seat behind me.

"Shut up," I barked.

I don't normally admonish strangers. It slipped out. When you are terrified of flying, the worst thing to hear is someone else doing the screaming, because it must mean we are *definitely* going down. Another ferocious rattle erupted and a bright white light flashed from outside.

"Lightning" volunteered the businessman beside me who was sitting bolt upright in his seat, his fingernails dug into the armrests. Not a word from the cockpit. The lightning flashed again. My heart was beating so hard I could almost hear it and my palms were drenched in sweat as I began to think of all I should have put straight if I had only known. There was another shudder and then finally a calm followed by an apology of sorts for the "slight turbulence".

I'd forgotten all about my terrifying arrival when I awoke to the sound of a speech being broadcast through a loudspeaker in

Spanish directly outside the hotel. I poked through the curtains but it was still night. The alarm clock by the bed said it was half past five. As my eyes adjusted, I made out a group of soldiers standing below in the middle of the huge square known as the Zocalo at the heart of Mexico City's historic district. The speech gave way to the head-wrecking sound of a bugle. Then a Mexican flag the size of a tennis court was hoisted up a flagpole. This was followed by another speech, not a word of which I understood, despite a rudimentary knowledge of Spanish. It didn't sound like a political rant, just an indecipherable monotone that echoed through the city centre until daylight, when it just stopped. "Oh they do that every morning," the concierge downstairs confirmed, indicating that daily flag-raising ceremonies were commonplace throughout Mexico.

Mexico City, one of the most populous cities in the world, is home to twenty million people. The central area is divided into zones, all with their own identities: the Zona Rosa is for tourists; Polanco is the upmarket residential and shopping area; Chapultepec Park houses the anthropological and art museums. The centre is then ringed by vast slums — poor, although not nearly as desperate as I had seen in cities farther south such as Lima in Peru, where shanties stretch for miles in every direction. Far from being Americanised, Mexico City has a Spanish feel, with street vendors and café bars and statues of the Virgin Mary on every corner. Most Mexicans are Catholic and are devoted to the Virgin of Guadeloupe. The story goes that in the sixteenth century she twice appeared here requesting that a church be built near the site of the current basilica. During her second attempt to deliver her message she asked a local man to gather roses in his cloak and take them to the local bishop. When he opened his garment, the image of the dark-skinned virgin he had seen was right there on the cloth. Every day thousands file into the basilica to see the original cloak which is hanging above the altar. Despite a strong Catholic tradition, however, evangelical missionaries have attracted large numbers of Mexicans away from the church.

In Mexico City I met up with my sister Claire, who had arrived from London, and together we travelled to Chiapas, the home province of Victor from the Mexican restaurant back in Maryland. We flew first to Tuxla Guiterrez and began a long taxi journey that wound high up into the Sierra Madre mountain range. Up there the deprivation and hardship was stark. Elderly women with faces like dried-up prunes stared at us from the roadside. Tiny children walked barefoot on the gravel. There was some evidence still of the Zapatista revolution against the Mexican government. Several homes were decorated with political slogans. The brief revolt in 1984 on behalf of the indigenous people of this area had received considerable support from outside Mexico and, despite an ongoing ceasefire, there were still military checkpoints along some roads. Another war had also been noticed here. "No al Genocidio de Bush" was daubed in big black letters on a rock overlooking a mountain town, a blunt reminder that Mexicans had not supported America's war in Iraq. Mexico (along with Canada) may be America's closest neighbour but that didn't deter President Vicente Fox from opposing the US decision to go to war.

Our driver offered to take us to a quarry for a swim, so he could charge us a few more American dollars, but we politely declined and two bumpy hours later arrived in San Cristobal de las Casas, not far from the Guatemalan border. If this was where Victor was from, I was already envious.

San Cristobal is a picture-perfect city nestled in a green valley. Its buildings are low and colourful and the shiny cobblestone streets form a tight maze winding up through the surrounding hills. The air was thinner here because of the high altitude but it was fresh. Walking around the town square, I felt a tug at my jacket and looked down to find a tiny native Mexican girl in bare feet trying to sell me home-made crafts.

"No, gracias," I smiled at her, thinking that would get me off the hook.

"Quatro, diez pesos," she whimpered as she held up a bunch of plaited cotton bracelets. She had huge dark eyes, a round grubby face and she looked fed up. She reminded me of the Mexicans I had seen captured on the Arizona border as they attempted to flee this kind of poverty. San Cristobal was beautiful alright, but it was also easy to see why so many were leaving it so they could clean offices in American cities. Mexicans who could only make five dollars a day in San Cristobal could earn sixty dollars a day in the US. I handed the girl the ten pesos, about a dollar, she picked out four wrist bands for me and fled. I was to see her many times again in the coming days and had to keep showing her my colourful wrists to let her know I had sufficient bracelets but one morning she appeared with a new item, a plastic doll with a black balaclava mask. "Marcos," she told me. I knew that if I didn't buy, I would be in big trouble. She was selling "Subcomandante Marcos", the leader of the Zapatista rebellion and a regional hero in Chiapas. He cost me two dollars.

AS WELL AS BEING HOME TO REVOLUTIONARIES, Chiapas was and still is a key centre of the Mayan tradition. About ten miles out of San Cristobal we came to the village of Chamula where a religious festival was underway.

Our Mexican guide, Alex, explained that in Mayan culture there are eighteen months in a year, each twenty days long and then five extra days to make up three hundred and sixty-five. Being early February, we were in this five-day period when Mayans say the sun renews itself in order to light and heat the earth for another year. As we climbed a hill by the back of the town, shots rang out, startling our group, but revolutionaries were not to blame this time. "Fireworks," said Alex, pointing to a trail of white smoke in the sky. "They are talking to the gods." Mayans believe in human reincarnation and pray to the gods to free their friends and relatives from the underworld where they go after death. Outside one house a large group was gathered, men sitting in one corner chatting, women and children spread out on the grass preparing food. For the religious festival the men wore traditional dress, thick black woolly shawls and white hats, while the women wore indigo, pink, orange and turquoise.

Everywhere we turned there were greenish blue crosses, a common symbol of Mayan worship. Many Mexicans in Chamula still believe the sun moves around the earth and that man was created from an ear of corn. Creation itself, they reckon, began in 3014 BC when the galaxy and sun were aligned in a particular manner and the current phase of creation will end in December 2012.

"What then?" an American tourist asked.

"Nobody seems to know," answered Alex as he led us into the church at the centre of the town. Roughly the equivalent of a medium-sized Irish church, it was filled with lighted candles — thousands of them burning on the floor, on tables, on makeshift altars and on every available surface. Women were lighting more candles and fixing them to the floor with the melting wax. Some of the flames had merged into a larger fire and clouds of smoke were rising all through the building. Around the edges of the church, plaster saints and other religious figures were displayed in glass boxes: the Virgin de Magdalena, Martha and San Miguel Arcangel.

"They have their arms cut off; they are prisoners," said Alex. The locals believed that the saints had let the old church at the far side of town burn down, never thinking that the fire might have been caused by too many candles burning at once. The glass boxes were ringed with flashing fairy lights and taped xylophone music was playing, giving the church the feel of a smoky casino in a dungeon. As we walked around quietly, it was obvious that several private ceremonies were underway. One family had placed about a hundred candles on the ground in rows. Behind them they had lined up glass bottles of Coke and Fanta and a rum drink they call "posh". It tasted very sweet and quite strong and may have accounted for the large crowds gathering in the church. First they pray for cosmic harmony and then drink rum and Coke.

I stood in the middle of this and tried to offer a prayer, but it didn't feel right, as though it was not getting through to the right deity. Instead, I contemplated the sun and wondered whether it would show up in December 2012.

A shaman standing nearby rocked back and forth as he chanted and talked to the gods. I stood silently listening, marvelling at how yet another brand of faith was keeping a people going. It was all a far cry from Victor and the Mexican restaurant back in Maryland. This was the real Mexico, not just the margarita version.

Chamula, however, was struggling to hold on to its traditions and was caught up in religious strife. An American familiar with the situation explained that several hundred villagers had decided to break with the Mayan traditions and had adopted Protestant evangelism instead. The drinking culture associated with the Mayan rituals often led to violence and this had turned people off. The breakaways, however, had been run out of the village and were now eking out a meagre living, selling home-made garments and dolls around San Cristobal. Others, Alex confirmed, had already left for Mexico City and for America.

A FIVE-HOUR MINIBUS JOURNEY to and from the Mayan ruins at Palenque sounded uncomfortable but Claire and I agreed that we would probably regret it if we didn't go. At six o'clock the following morning the packed bus climbed out of San Cristobal, going so high that we were actually above the clouds. Along the road men with duffle bags waited to be picked up for work, children walked to school and women trudged along with bundles of sticks on their backs. We crawled up through little mountain towns where toddlers looked out from dark doorways and horses nibbled lazily at what the jungle had to offer at the side of the road. The houses were made of adobe or wood and were impossibly small for the extended families sheltering in them. Every dwelling looked unfinished with steel rods jutting up from the roof as if an upper storey had yet to be added. But there was little construction going on and most roofs were being used to dry clothes or to grow exotic flowers for the markets.

Any interest in the passing scene gradually faded as nausea crept up on me. The road had become interminably twisted. Stuck in a minibus with a dozen tourists, none of whom were yet speaking to each other, we were thrown from one side of the seat to the other with every bend. I was about to ask the driver to stop when the bus pulled in, depositing us at a roadside tortilla joint for breakfast. Everyone else on the bus ate heartily. My sister and I stayed outside, sitting with our heads between our knees. Back on the bus, as we continued to be jolted around, I listened to a pair of Australian girls attempting to make conversation with a couple of Italians. All of us tourists were in the same linguistically challenged boat, having little more than phrasebook Spanish. With the help of some patchy translation and sign language, the Australians managed to ascertain that the two Italians were policemen from Sicily. One of the Australians got excited as she disclosed that her mother was Italian but couldn't remember which town she was from. She had not been back to Italy in thirty years. "T-r-e-i-n-t-a" she emphasised with three fingers up. The Italians nodded and suggested a few towns but she rejected all of them. "Nah, not that wan. It'll come to me layda."

Not wishing to give up yet on the Sicilian policemen, she tried switching topics. "Oh, ya know, oi werk nee the outlet for Lambageenee."

The Sicilians stared blankly at the Australian.

"Lam-ba-gee-nee," she tried again emphasising each syllable. The cops looked at one another and back at her as the minibus swerved around a corner, throwing us all sharply to the right and back again. Everyone else on the bus except the Italians knew what she was talking about and started tittering.

"Kah," she added by way of further translation, jabbing her finger towards the road.

"Ahhhhhh, Lamborghini," gushed the two policemen in unison, "aaahh si, si." That appeared to be the end of the conversation because neither party had the vocabulary to continue but the Australian then announced that she used to work for Audi. I felt another wave of nausea and knew that the only thing I wanted to hear about vehicles right now was when I'd be getting out of this particular one.

Several hours and three pit stops later, we arrived at Palenque on the edge of the Yucatán plain. As we entered the site, massive tiered pyramids loomed up from the jungle where they had remained hidden for centuries before being discovered by a priest in 1790. Ongoing excavations had revealed the tombs of Mayan leaders dating back to 100 BC. These elevated burial chambers still contained items that had been placed with the deceased for their journey to Xibalba, the Mayan underworld. There were jewels, weapons and utensils for food and drink.

We climbed scores of steep steps, reaching the top of the Temple of the Sun and looked across at the Temple of the Inscriptions where tourists appeared as tiny specks advancing upwards. Palenque was once the seat of power in Chiapas province, flourishing in the seventh century under two men whose names translate as Jaguar Shield and Jaguar Serpent. Fourteen hundred years on, we panted in the heat as we investigated each nook and cranny of these sacred structures. Howler monkeys hiding in the trees screeched, supplying an eerie soundtrack.

BUT YOU CAN'T EAT SCENERY or culture or religion and for that reason Victor and so many other modern Mexicans are leaving this mystical place for the roadside restaurants of Maryland and New Jersey and the rest of the United States. In America, immigrants live apart from the mainstream, sometimes hidden from view. They have their share of trouble and recently a re-formed Ku Klux Klan has been making noises about keeping Hispanics out of America.

Victor seemed more than a little homesick when I showed him my photographs back at the Mexican restaurant off Route 50. He recognised almost everything in them, including the church at Chamula and the town square in San Cristobal.

"There's my sister on the Templo del Sol," I pointed out the tiny figure halfway up the immense stone monument.

"Ah Palenque, you liked it?"

"Very much so," I said as I tried to suppress memories of the bus trip that had rendered me greener than the guacamole on the table in front of me.

Chapter 8

Faith, Oil and Charity

$\mathcal{F}$OR ME, TEXAS IS ONE of America's most interesting states. Geographically it is huge. Roughly the size of France, it runs eight hundred miles from one side to the other. Its land is mainly flat with wide vistas topped off by an endless sky, the exception being the rolling hill country around San Antonio and Austin. Tucked up against the Mexican border, the southern part of the state has a Spanish feel and plays host to plenty of frontier shenanigans, while along the Gulf of Mexico the state has hundreds of miles of coastline and sandy beaches. Texas is mainly about cattle ranching and oil drilling, both outdoor activities, yet it is hotter than hell for much of the year. But the Lone Star State also has a heartbeat, an internal rhythm all its own which makes it feel like a separate country. Not isolated, just different, and most definitely not dull.

My first foray into Texas was on a solo mission to report from the Republican convention in Houston, way back in 1992. George

H.W. Bush was President, facing a challenge from a little-known entity from Arkansas, Bill Clinton. My hotel in Houston was described as being in the city, so after checking in I set off on foot for the downtown area. After thirty minutes the tall buildings I had seen looming to the east were no closer and the footpath had disappeared, forcing me to walk on the grass verge beside the highway. Every now and then, a car horn would sound and when I looked around I would invariably find someone waving and smiling at me. These Texans sure were friendly. Eventually a car pulled up and a policeman with a gun strapped to his waist got out.

"Are you OK, Ma'am?"

"Just heading into town."

"Get in," he said, giving me a look that said, "You're not from around here are you?" The policeman explained that no one walked anywhere in Texas. What's more, the only women to be found wandering on the side of the road were soliciting for business. He gave me his card and indicated that, if I needed to get someplace else during my stay, I should call him before attempting to walk.

Downtown Houston turned out to be a lifeless concrete jungle with barely a single shop or even a place to get a Coke. I returned to the hotel in a taxi.

Because of the nature of my mission, which was to broadcast reports from the convention back to Ireland at four o'clock in the morning, I spent a lot of time awake at night and sleeping by day. I would hit the convention for the speeches in the evening, wander off to some young Republicans' event for a few hours and then get to work. As I recall it, the Republican delegates were a lot more fun back then and alcohol flowed freely at these parties. Today, iced tea is the drink of choice for all political operatives. The 1992 convention did not go all that well for George Bush Sr. His Vice Presidential running mate, Dan Quayle, was considered a lightweight and Quayle's wife Marilyn gave a speech about family values that was received as being much too conservative for the times! Bush went on to lose the election to Clinton.

On my last day in Houston, I awoke around lunchtime to the sound of screaming from the next room. I couldn't make out any verbal exchanges, but it did sound like a struggle was taking place with a woman at the centre of it. I banged on the wall but the noise worsened. I tried calling the front desk but there was no answer. I sprinted to the lobby. It was deserted. Panicking, I felt I had no choice but to call the police before someone was murdered. I fled back to my room and, just to kill the noise of the struggle, I flicked on the TV. I jumped. Suddenly the commotion was now in my room. The screaming and shouting I had heard was coming from the television — the pornography channel.

I HAD GAINED A LOT MORE SENSE when I made my next solo trip to Texas thirteen years later. This time, I knew enough to rent a car and avoid cheap motels. What had not changed was the reason for my visit. I was in the town of Midland and again it was because of a member of the Bush family.

Midland is a miniature version of Houston. Nicknamed "The Tall City", it is a small cluster of high-rise buildings, surrounded by fairly plain residential neighbourhoods and some seedy-looking commercial strips. I checked in to an inn and for old times' sake went exploring on foot. Only this time, to avoid any confusion, I changed into running clothes and jogged towards downtown. For at least twenty minutes I passed nothing other than car dealerships. In America, cars are sold from huge lots on the side of the road, each lot decorated with more bunting and American flags than the last. To say that they were dealing in cars is not entirely accurate. No one in Midland drives a car. You get around in a truck and not just your average SUV. Here they drive super-sized flatbeds with V8 cylinder engines and leather seats the size of armchairs. I passed a roadside store called "Larry's Discount Smokes". Outside it a scantily dressed Hispanic girl of about fifteen was enjoying the advances of an older black male. Eventually she ran away across a parking lot, waving goodbye to him, but he chased after her and they disappeared down the road together. I ran past the usual selection of fast food restaurants and a bar with a neon sign that read "Your Place". Half the town seemed to be parked outside but I saw nobody either enter or leave.

The Bush neighbourhood, just a short distance away, is a lot more respectable — the kind of place where kids can safely ride their bikes to school and play baseball. The gardens are manicured and the bungalows — though probably the height of modernity when the Bushes lived here — now seemed outdated.

Though George W. Bush was born in Connecticut in 1946, his parents George and Barbara moved to Midland when their son was still a toddler. The house George W. grew up in is nothing much to look at. It's a small grey clapboard home in a quiet neighbourhood on the edge of town. Down the street a few blocks, there is a second house where he lived and a few streets over a third. Around the corner and over a few streets more, there is a fourth where he and Laura started out married life. By the time I arrived in Midland, the most modest-looking of the houses had been taken over by a local conservation group which was in the process of restoring it to how it was in the 1950s when the President was a boy.

"The first time I saw him, he was playing catcher for the Cubs. He was dressed in red," Don Poage told me, pointing to the fields where he and George W. Bush played little league as kids. Don, who has lived in Midland all his life, is roughly the same age as Bush. "My sister liked him and that meant he was cool, so I wanted to be a catcher too." The young Bush attended the local elementary and high schools, both still operating today, and went to Sunday school at the Presbyterian Church with his parents. It all looks very normal and a tad dull. But this is where the forty-third president of the United States was shaped. This is the town where as a boy he lost his baby sister to cancer and where he met his wife and raised his own family. It is also the place where he searched for oil but found religion.

LISTENING TO PRESIDENT BUSH back in Washington, I could sometimes close my eyes and imagine I was in a church. Following his words and deeds through the tragedy of September 11th, the bitter clash with the United Nations and the war in Iraq, the question I most often wrestled with was whether or not he believed he was on a God-given mission, and it was the one question I immediately knew I wanted to ask him when I interviewed him. In justifying his most controversial actions, he regularly speaks of freedom as a gift to the world from the "Almighty". He also claims to serve a higher power, something greater than himself. George Bush is eager to label everything in sight as either good or evil. He is seldom short of Biblical references and more often than not the rhetoric of his key speeches is so firmly rooted in scripture and faith that it is difficult to distinguish the politics from the preaching. I believe that no one can question the personal faith of another. But George Bush was elected to be a president, not a pastor. I had often found myself wondering if this deference to the Almighty was genuinely at the core of this former oilman or if his piety was simply a convenient crowd-pleaser. His home town seemed like a good place to search for clues.

The town used to be called Midway — the halfway point along the railroad from Fort Worth to El Paso near the Mexican border. In the 1920s oil had been discovered in west Texas. By the next boom twenty years later, roughnecks from the country and educated types from the east coast were converging on Midland and nearby Odessa in order to cash in. There are streets in Midland named after Princeton and Harvard, apparently because so many of their graduates ended up there. George Herbert Walker Bush came with little money and, judging by the houses I saw, lived fairly frugally. But he wasn't exactly a nonentity. By the time he arrived in Midland, he was a Yale law graduate, a decorated World

War II hero and the son of successful senator and businessman Prescott Bush. Like everybody else, George Bush Sr had come to this hot dusty place to find oil.

West Texas is located in what geologists call the Permian Basin, an area that at several times in history was under water. Some believe oil may have formed from decayed animal matter, trapped at points where the rocks fractured far below ground. Finding oil has always been a gambler's game. The prospector must first bore thousands of feet into the ground at a cost of millions of dollars. Even with modern geological knowledge, there is still only a one in fifteen chance of striking it lucky. Then, the oil has to be slowly drawn out of the depths like you would suck liquid through a straw. George Bush Sr got lucky. He made his money, and when George W. was a teenager, dad said goodbye to Midland and moved the family to Houston.

But that was not the end of the Midland connection. George W. Bush called it home and, after he had followed his father's footsteps to Yale, he returned to the west Texas town. By the time he came back in the 1970s, Midland had become the official centre of the local oil business and one in every forty inhabitants was a millionaire.

"I would see him at John and Jan O'Neill's house," said Don Poage. "We shared a couple of oil deals and played some tennis. He was a good player." The O'Neills, a prominent Midland couple, liked to throw barbecues in their backyard and it was at their home that Bush met librarian Laura Welsh. At the time, the price of oil was rising fast, jumping first from three dollars up to ten dollars a barrel and eventually all the way up to forty dollars. "They were wild times," recalled Don Poage, who said the success often brought with it heavy drinking, drug abuse and divorces. Being a dry county, there were no bars in Midland, so everyone went to Odessa to party. "They used to say you raised your family in Midland but you raised hell in Odessa!" Don laughed. To beat the ban, private clubs sprang up. The most notable of these was Midland's

Petroleum Club which is still in the centre of town. "We all drank," said Poage, with a glint in his eye. He hinted that some people also dabbled in drugs but believes George Bush did not. "I would have known about it if he did."

Don Poage is slim and healthy-looking, with a friendly smile and a big heart. When we met he was dressed casually in jeans and a polo shirt, the unofficial uniform in Midland. "Coco," he greeted me; I was surprised that he had managed to extract my nickname from an e-mail address. After giving me a tour of the town, he brought me to a Mexican restaurant where we talked about family, politics and George Bush.

I didn't expect to hear any dark secrets about the President. Midlanders are intensely proud of him and Texans stick together. Neither did I expect to be casually introduced to a woman who had once dated Bush. An attractive blonde stopped by our table to greet Don. The dating was mentioned in passing for my benefit. As a journalist, I am always looking for a story, but this didn't seem like the time or place to be asking a middle-aged woman if the President had been a good kisser. I remarked that she looked a bit young for him, which she took as a compliment before excusing herself. Don Poage's own life in Midland had been a series of ups and downs. He used to be a drinker but had not touched a drink in twenty-two years. He had made some decent money from oil but had searched for something more significant and personally satisfying. Now he was counselling youngsters who were having problems with drugs and alcohol. Like the President, he had undergone a transformation in his life. That is, he and George Bush and half of Midland.

KELLY COLEMAN, A WELL-GROOMED MAN in his fifties, had sandy hair and a neat moustache. Though he shares my surname, bears a slight resemblance to an uncle of mine and his people did come from England, we could find no further evidence that we were related. He is in the Christian missionary business, and at his downtown office was working on a project to put Christian radio stations into Sudan.

"We are trying to evangelise Christians there," he said, explaining that this means helping them get saved, then following up rapidly with Bible classes broadcast over the radio in their native language. "We can get a radio station up in two days that reaches a hundred thousand people." From a drawer in his desk Kelly took a small portable radio set powered by a solar panel and fixed to just one frequency — his frequency. Following the instruction in the Bible to "go into the world and teach all nations", he had already distributed these radios in several countries. Made especially for the evangelical market, the radio was called a "Go-Ye"!

Kelly Coleman was not just in the business of converting others. He too had a personal story.

"After high school I became hooked on cocaine and alcohol, and wound up in rehab in Houston," he told me. As he spoke, I noticed he had one of those deep baritone radio voices with the authority to make you sit up and listen. Looking at Kelly, it was hard to picture him strung out on drugs and booze, but then most of America's baby-boom generation had tried something illegal. Many of them had gone on to become today's liberals, but not those in Midland, Texas.

"I was rescued by some Christian businessmen here in town. I received the power of the Holy Spirit and that changed my life completely," Coleman announced, confirming that, just like Don Poage and George Bush, faith had intervened to snatch him from oblivion. But this outburst of divinity in 1980s' Midland didn't just come from nowhere. The oil, it seemed, had been responsible for it. Back then the talk was that the price of a barrel might go all the way to seventy dollars. According to resident Margaret Purvis, the banks sent sales people onto the streets of Midland to give loans away to anyone who wanted to take a chance on finding oil. Everyone did. Kelly Coleman was a "land man", the person who finds out who owns the land, then leases it for drilling. Oil, however, didn't go up to seventy dollars a barrel; instead in 1986 the price collapsed, and with it the First National Bank of Midland. "The bank used to be in this building where we are now," Coleman said, looking out on Midland's very own deserted Wall Street.

Kelly came across George W. Bush at a Bible study group, which got its start in 1986, just after the big downturn. "Community Bible Study", a programme for examining the scriptures, had been devised by women in Washington DC. The first men's chapter of the programme was established in Midland. After the collapse a lot of local men realised that there must be more to life than oil. In search of something more meaningful, over two hundred of Midland's businessmen turned to God.

George Bush Sr had not passed on the Midas touch to his son. George W's oil company, Arbusto, was jokingly referred to around Midland as "Arbusted"! Not only that, he lost his first chance at election for a seat in the Texas state government. His father's luck and ambition, however, never ran out. Bush Sr had become a United States Senator, head of the CIA, and Ambassador to China. By now he was Vice President of the United States, serving with Ronald Reagan, and was deciding to make a run for President.

Back in Midland, his son George W. was giving up beer and finding Jesus. "I used to run into him in the hall," Kelly Coleman told me, recalling the Bible study nights. Kelly had campaigned locally for a rival candidate, the prominent evangelist Pat Robertson, but he claims George W. only teased him about it. "He'd say, 'Kelly, don't tell anyone, but I'm really voting for Pat Robertson myself!'" The Bible study was intensive, focusing on one gospel for an entire year. "The first year we studied Luke," said Coleman. "I thought, man . . . I had no idea it was so deep, we would study one verse for three hours."

Don Poage, who had stopped visiting the bars, was also in the Bible class and remembers Bush. "George was self-effacing and very off-the-cuff," he said, recalling the Monday nights they spent dissecting psalms and verses instead of football scores. According to

Don, W. always presented himself as just one of the gang but it was the small things that set the Vice President's son apart. "One night we had been talking about how Jesus said to Nicodemus that you must be born again. The next week he came back and said he had got his mother to phone Billy Graham to see if that was true . . . I mean, imagine just picking up the phone to Billy Graham!"

By now George was saved. "Don Evans led him to the Lord," Kelly Coleman told me, referring to another prominent Midland businessman. Whatever spiritual conversion Midland underwent in the 1980s, it seemed to have a lasting effect. Two decades on, George W. Bush was President of the United States, Kelly Coleman and Don Poage had found ways to make their lives significant in Midland, and all three were still sober.

SO IT WAS ICED TEAS ALL ROUND as we sat down to lunch in Midland's Petroleum Club, the same establishment where the drinking had been done in the wild days. The Petroleum Club looks like a fine hotel. In a downstairs room Midland's Mayor was attending a function while upstairs a large dining room was full of people who looked as though they had made a few dollars from the oil business. I almost expected to bump into Jock Ewing or Sue Ellen from *Dallas*. There was a buzz about the place, and no wonder. After years of stagnation, a sharp price rise had got the oil industry moving again in Midland. "Oh, there's still oil here," said Kelly Coleman, explaining that the problem now was a shortage of drilling machinery. Old oil wells, closed up when prices collapsed, were almost impossible to reopen. So prospectors were back to drilling holes and taking gambles. While instability in the Middle East and the growing energy demand from China brought only bad news to everyone else, you got the feeling that Midland was looking forward to a taste of the old glory days.

By now, Kelly, Don and myself had been joined by Deborah Fikes, a top Midland Republican. Deborah is the type of woman who makes an impression when entering a room. She wore a stylish dark suit and high heels. She looked as though she had just come straight from a salon, with her big Texas-style blonde hair. Her makeup was applied liberally and she looked much younger than her forty-nine years. Between taking mobile phone calls, she explained in her very slow and precise southern way that it was both George Bush's and Midland's destiny to serve those in need. She was part of the "Ministerial Alliance", a group of local leaders helping persecuted Christians around the world. From what I had seen so far, Midland was a hotbed of Christian outreach. Kelly Coleman, who was listening, agreed that there was something uncommon about Midland. A preacher from England named Derek Prince, he claimed, had predicted several years earlier that Midland would become a staging ground for world evangelism.

George Bush may have heard that story, too. By the mid-1990s he had learned his Bible and formed relationships with evangelical groups, worked on his father's presidential campaign, bought a baseball team and got himself elected Governor of Texas. Governor Bush maintained his contacts with evangelists Billy Graham and James Robson and confided to them that he felt he was being "called" to run for President. That is, called by God. In his autobiography, *A Charge to Keep*, George Bush recalls listening to a Dallas pastor talk about Moses. Initially reluctant to lead God's people, Moses went on to deliver the Jews from slavery in Egypt. George Bush remembers the pastor saying that Americans were starved of leaders with ethical and moral courage. Sitting in church that day, he felt the message was directed towards him. As if to confirm it, the autobiography recounts how his mother Barbara turned to him afterwards and said, "He was talking to you, George."

A lot of water has since passed under the bridge. As I picked at my shrimp salad at the Petroleum Club, surrounded on all sides by the President's strongest supporters, I couldn't help reminding my lunch companions that much of the world still considered Bush to be an oil-grabbing maniac, with a poor command of the English language and no moral conscience. They were all quite aware of this image and were certain that it was my fault — mine and the rest of the media.

Don Poage, who up to now had been eating his steak, dropped his fork to get in on this. Almost ninety per cent of the American press, he claimed, had supported Al Gore in 2000. The media was an entrenched system, just like college professors who he felt were still trying to push the Marxist ideals of big government, higher taxes and the redistribution of wealth. As we talked and ate, the cultural and spiritual battle raging across the country was starting to get nasty. President Bush was trying to get conservative judges on the Supreme Court and Democrats were doing all they could to stop him. Americans were bickering over public use of religious symbols and references. They were obsessing over how the world got started, and disagreeing over whether or not charities should be given public money to deliver salvation or soup.

In Midland, the feeling was that conservatives were not to blame for these clashes. Stirring the pot were groups like the American Civil Liberties Union which, George Bush's former neighbours claimed, always backed liberals against conservative Christians. But even more than journalists, professors or the ACLU, the most serious threat to American values were liberal judges — judges who, the Midlanders felt, were making laws that did not befit a Christian nation.

"In 1973 with *Roe v. Wade* they made up a huge policy that never existed," said Don Poage, referring to the Supreme Court ruling that made abortion legal in America. "We were told it was about making it clean, neat, safe and rare. Well now we are up to a million and a half a year. You know what's wrong with social security? We are missing forty million workers. We killed them," he stated emotionally, looking clearly distressed.

Deborah Fikes wanted to get in on this one and she was whispering. "That's also why the Democratic Party is declining in voters. You have a generation that probably would have been more in that party's demographic but they have been aborted." For a moment or two she seemed a bit embarrassed that she had said this, but the others were all nodding, so I just kept writing.

They had provided some answers for me. I now had a sense of the tough-minded place where George W. Bush had grown up and I knew how direct Midlanders could be. I was still trying to work out the extent to which he allowed his faith to do the governing. The US appears to be splitting nervously between those who believe that Christian principles deserve a central place in public life and those who fear America is headed towards a theocracy, a government by God. Those who knew George Bush, although very casually, didn't think there was any danger of that. "He can talk about his personal faith but he hasn't imposed it on others," Deborah Fikes believed, dismissing with a wave of her hand any notion that Bush was being led by the Christian right. "If we pulled his strings the way the press portrays it, he would be very different on gay marriage," she added, stressing that the President, in recently released private recordings, had stated that he would refuse to "kick gays". Those with greater access to the President believe his views on social issues are not nearly as strong as the conservative right would like. While he may not be able or willing to deliver all their demands, putting a conservative judge on the Supreme Court is likely to be the big payback for those who elected him.

WE WERE THE LAST PEOPLE LEFT in the dining room at the Petroleum Club. We had been talking for two hours and I hadn't even reached the subject of Iraq.

"Are you happy with how the war is going?" I asked those around the table.

Don Poage immediately chastised me for asking the question. "I hate war. That's like asking Franklin Roosevelt if he's happy with the bomb over Hiroshima. Sometimes I think presidents have to make decisions that are unbelievably difficult." Using a pocket mirror to check her makeup, Deborah Fikes assured me that Midland was not cracking on this issue. "The general consensus you would get from the Midland community is that it was a just war," she said. For her, Saddam Hussein was the real weapon of mass destruction. He was reason enough to go to war.

President Bush had tried to convince the world that the invasion of Iraq was not about oil and not about religion — the two most important commodities in Midland. If not faith or oil, could it have been about charity? Not having found weapons of mass destruction, he wanted Americans to accept that it was about giving Iraqis the gift of freedom and democracy. But it was hard to believe that nothing was expected in return. In his second inaugural speech the President had stated that America's beliefs and interests were now one. The very least the neo-conservatives could expect in return for this freedom was an Iraq more hospitable towards the US and more willing and able to accept investments from American oil companies.

Almost three years into the war, it didn't look great. Those fighting against the occupation were still making America feel unwelcome and the price of oil, instead of coming down, had shot up, heading towards the all-time highs that Midland had dreamed of back in the 1980s.

It is also hard to accept that faith had no part to play in it. The personal image George Bush has created by wearing his faith on his sleeve netted him as many votes in 2004 than any single issue or decision he ever made in office. Likewise, by claiming that there is some higher purpose in prosecuting the war on terror, he has kept some Americans on board who might otherwise have deserted the ship long ago. Others, convinced that he is using religion to serve his own political ends, can only laugh at the idea that God might somehow be sanctioning a war that apparently has no end. The view among liberals, even those who believe in God, is that to invoke a higher power as a back-up for foreign policy decisions is plain wrong. Yet that is what George Bush did right after September 11th 2001, when he told Congress that America was at war. "The course of this conflict is not known, yet its outcome is certain. Freedom and fear, justice and cruelty have always been at war and we know that God is not neutral between them," he said. It sounded as though he was claiming to know how God felt about the situation. Taken together with his earlier belief that he was being "called" to run for the presidency, one could not help but wonder if one of the Oval Office telephones was hooked up to the Almighty.

I had set out for Texas with a view that George Bush was genuinely a God-fearing man and nothing I heard in Midland disabused me of that notion. Yet I still didn't know whether he was using God or God was using him.

"He's a good man," Kelly Coleman stated simply, when we finally turned to the subject of George and the higher powers. "I think he's a real man of integrity and he has come under tremendous flak. You know, Jesus said: 'They'll hate you because they hated me first.'" Don Poage nodded. Bush didn't give a hoot whether people agreed with him or not, so long as he was convinced he was doing the right thing. For me, this was the nub of the mystery. George Bush seemed to be permanently gripped by an absolute certainty that he was doing the right thing. Coming as he did from the oil business, where a prospector only had a one in fifteen chance of being right, this seemed very strange. Could it be that he did have doubts about his decisions to send Americans to war in Afghanistan or Iraq, but kept these doubts to himself? Or was he still a gambling man who had factored in the belief that, with the Almighty on his side, surely the odds of things turning out well had to be better than one in fifteen? When I had met him in the White House Library, he did say that he prayed for forgiveness, perhaps an indication that Bush recognised he was sometimes wrong. We may never know. Whatever the truth, those I met in Texas were sure that his religious awakening, right there in Midland, was playing a significant role in his presidency.

"The transformation in his life has given him much more purpose than he would have had if that transformation had not occurred. You take a man who had not been successful in busi-ness, whose marriage was in trouble and who had a drinking prob-lem — and decided, 'Something's got to change in my life' . . . I think he's someone who thinks he has been given a lot and can use it for good," Deborah Fikes elaborated before picking up the tab and disappearing out the door.

THREE DAYS AFTER I LEFT MIDLAND, I realised that I had missed Laura Bush, who, according to the local paper, had been there to visit her mother. The article said that as she drove past a local school she had seen dozens of old school desks in the yard waiting to be dumped. Mrs Bush had called the local authority to retrieve the desks and had made arrangements to have them sent to a school in Afghanistan. Again this was one of those moments when the sceptic in me had to take a break. Clearly there was something special about Midland.

I had learned a bit about the oil business and before leaving I cruised around to see the pump jacks bobbing up and down in the fields. At the Petroleum Museum, I wandered through exhibits sponsored by Halliburton and passed portraits of the great oil men. Among them was George Bush Sr. His accompanying biography mentioned his various oil interests and former partners and almost as an afterthought referenced the fact that he had served as Presi-dent of the United States. George W. Bush didn't crack the oil busi-ness in Midland and might never get his picture up here, but most of the world still regards him as Bush the Texas oilman.

On the way out of town I stopped off at "Your Place", the bar I had passed the first night. There were three cowboys sitting up at the counter watching a baseball game on television. Every head turned when I entered. They didn't say it, but I knew what they were thinking as they eyed me. "Hey girl, you're not from around here, are you?"

Chapter 9

Striving in the Cause of Allah

*I*T WAS EARLY MORNING as the ferry moved across the bay headed for what looked like a tropical island. The sun was already blazing, its rays spreading a golden shimmer on the water. Around the boat seagulls hovered, swooping and diving at intervals for the small fish that inhabit the warm waters of the Caribbean.

"Welcome to the Pearl of the Antilles."

That's what the air stewardess had said when our plane landed back on the far side of the bay. Maybe that's how this spot is known to sailors who skirt by here, careful not to drift too close. To the rest of the world, it is better known as Guantanamo Bay.

"Welcome to Gitmo."

The military welcoming committee, Colonel Johnson and Lieutenant Moss, extended firm handshakes to cameraman Harvey Cofske and myself, and to a film crew from *Sky News*. "Gitmo" is military slang for the US naval base located on the south-east corner of Cuba. For over a hundred years America has held an indefinite lease on the land in exchange for an annual sum of five thousand dollars. Fidel Castro has never bothered cashing the cheques and would rather see Uncle Sam pack up and go home. Until early 2002, America used the base to detain illegal migrants from Cuba and Haiti and, no doubt, to keep an eye on the communist comings and goings on the far side of the fence, but outside of military circles, few had ever heard of Guantanamo Bay. By the time I got there in the summer of 2003, it had been reborn as one of the most notorious prison camps on earth.

From the time the US invaded Afghanistan, hundreds of Muslim men, captured as enemies of America, had been shipped halfway around the world to Gitmo. Still reeling from the attacks of September 11th, the Bush administration declared the men to be "enemy combatants" — often religious fanatics with no insignia on their uniform and therefore not entitled to the rights generally accorded to prisoners of war. This was one of the events that woke up the world to the fact that America had changed. The very idea that a democracy would depart from the status quo on human rights in its own backyard sent shockwaves around the globe. As a damage limitation exercise, foreign media, including RTÉ, were granted permission to visit the prison camp.

We had already checked in to our military accommodation on a strip of sun-scorched earth known simply as the Leeward Side. My assigned quarters took me back to my boarding school days. Other than four single beds, a closet and a toilet, the room was bare. But it was still the cheapest accommodation I had stayed in in years. The Pentagon charged just $16 a night to civilian visitors, and this included breakfast in the mess hall at six in the morning with everyone else.

Amid the hubbub of settling in and the jokes about watching out for tarantulas in the bed, I had temporarily let go of the mental picture I carried of the prisoners in orange jumpsuits, shackled and blindfolded. Now, as we approached the camp itself, I came swiftly back to my senses. At first sight, Camp Delta didn't look like much. The single-storey structure was completely surrounded by a fence and covered by a dark green tarpaulin to frustrate prying cameras. When the first prisoners had arrived it was appropriately called Camp X-ray, because you could see right inside. Now all that was visible were the guard towers, tall wooden structures wrapped in layers of barbed wire and bristling with telescopes, searchlights and night-vision equipment.

It would be pretty much impossible to escape from here. The only way to leave Gitmo is to swim or to make a dash into Cuba. The US coastguard constantly patrols the waters and the Cuban border, which runs along the hills behind the prison, is fenced off and heavily guarded on both sides.

"Please do not film the faces of anyone entering or leaving the camp," Lieutenant Moss asked as we approached the main entrance. Prison guards and interrogators, we were told, did not want their pictures broadcast for fear of reprisals. There was a constant stream of people entering and leaving by the front gate; some turned their heads away from us, while others just walked past our cameras, trusting that we would not step out of line.

I don't think I have ever been to a place as brutally hot as Guantanamo. The day we arrived, the temperature was about one hundred and six degrees Fahrenheit and, even with a steady supply of iced water and plenty of opportunities to take shade, getting around was difficult. We would be on the base for just three days but being posted here for any length of time seemed like a punishment in itself. Guantanamo Bay may have looked like a paradise island from the ferry boat but on closer inspection it was more like a little corner of hell, and that was just the outside.

Young prison guards who had been lined up to talk to us did what they are supposed to do. They reassured us. Everything inside Camp Delta, they said, was running smoothly and they were all proud to do their bit for the war on terror. A confident African American woman of about twenty explained it from her point of view: "I don't make things hard for myself, but I don't make things easy for the detainees either. As long as they co-operate with me, I co-operate with them and we get the job done."

Later that night as we headed back to our sleeping quarters, and the cameras were off, I overheard the other side of the story.

"I wish I could get out of this fucking hell-hole," a female soldier complained to her colleagues. She was due to serve out a year at Gitmo, but there was nothing to do outside of work, it was too hot and the place only ever got rotten publicity. If the food was anything to go by, she had probably also lost the use of her taste buds by the time she left. In the mess hall, the lamb chops were like old boot leather and full of small sharp splinters of bone. But everyone was lapping them up without complaint. I suppose you just get used to it.

THE FOLLOWING MORNING WE WERE BACK in front of Camp Delta, and this time we were going inside. Colonel Adolph McQueen, a tall black man running this part of the operation, met us at the main entrance. We passed through a huge gate, which was manned by several soldiers. Colonel McQueen opened a second gate, and this too slammed shut and was locked as we entered through yet a third. Clunk. Creak. Bang. The last gate closed behind us.

The first stop inside Camp Delta was an empty cell block in the maximum security area. Each cell was tiny, with just enough room for a bed and some space to stand, and maybe swing your arms. Each one had a hole in the floor (an Asian toilet) and a washbasin. The cells were constructed out of thick wire mesh and it was almost as hot inside as out in the open air.

"This block is equipped with all the comfort items we provide to detainees within the camp who have shown us positive behaviour," Colonel McQueen spoke slowly as he listed the perks. "They get long pants, a top, two towels, a face cloth, prayer beads, a prayer cap and a Qur'an." He indicated an arrow on the wall, which pointed to the south-west. Underneath it was written "Mecca, 12,973 kilometers"; thus, inmates would know which direction to face as they prayed to their holy of holies five times a day.

We were joined by Lieutenant John VanNatta, a security expert seconded to Camp Delta from a prison in Indiana, who confirmed that communal praying was a constant activity in the camp, day and night. "It's like a chant or a song; one chants something, and the others repeat it. It goes back and forth like that, and it's quite loud," he said, hinting that he would prefer to be listening to something else. But it also had its upside. Praying kept the detainees occupied — when they weren't being interrogated. It had never been suggested that they had been prevented from worshipping; the military played a recorded call to prayer five times a day. But there were deep religious sensitivities involved. Allegations that a copy of the Qur'an had been flushed down a toilet would later spark deadly riots in Afghanistan in 2005. The Pentagon quickly denied the claim and *Newsweek* magazine, which had published the allegation, withdrew its story. Yet three Britons freed in 2004 after two years in captivity had made the very same claim. In hindsight, it was easy to see how any object in the tiny cells could, with a kick or a shove, have landed in the Asian toilet, but proving that it had been done intentionally would be impossible.

At the bottom end of the cell block there was a small outdoor area. Co-operative detainees were taken there for thirty minutes a day to kick a ball or exercise. They could then shower for five minutes and shave for another five. Anyone suspected of holding back valuable information was allowed out of their cell only twice a week, for a total of one hour.

"So where are they all now?" I asked Colonel McQueen, wondering why the place was so quiet. There is always shouting and yelling in prisons but this one was eerily silent. It was, of course, a stupid question. The empty cell block was just for the likes of me and other media sceptics. The high-security detainees were in other blocks throughout the camp, but we would not be seeing them. The only people allowed to have any contact with the men were the prison staff, the interrogators and (occasionally) the Red Cross. There was no visiting, no phone calls, and no post in or out of Camp Delta. To the rest of the world the prisoners were unidentified and incommunicado.

I did see some of the medium security prisoners. Deemed to be co-operating sufficiently with their captors, these were housed in a separate section. "Even if they shout out to you, you must ignore them," the Colonel warned us, making it clear that disobeying this command would terminate our visit immediately. We were taken past what looked like a fenced-in patio. About ten dark figures dressed in dazzling white tunics sat at tables on the patio. Some of the men were peeling oranges and others were playing a board game. They all had jet black hair and long beards and they looked healthy. The scene was almost biblical, as if we were watching courtiers in some distant Arab land relaxing in the shade. As we were moved on past them, some of the detainees did stare back at us, one glanced in my direction and then quickly averted his eyes again, but no one made any attempt to call out to us. I can only imagine what they thought, but I felt like a visitor at a zoo.

In a prefabricated hut near the soldiers' dormitories, we met Captain James Yee. An army chaplain, Yee was one of the media stars of Camp Delta. An American of Asian descent, he had converted to Islam — a Muslim soldier ministering to Muslim detainees. Harvey set up the camera and I interrogated him, hoping he might reveal some sense of what was going on in the minds of the prisoners — but of course he couldn't say anything other than that there were no problems in the camp and he was proud to serve. His main concern was getting a copy of our television report.

"I'll mail it to you," I promised.

"All reporters say they will, but they forget," he said.

"I promise I won't forget."

I never did send the tape to Chaplain Yee. Not long after our visit he was removed from his posting and placed under investigation. From what I could gather he was suspected of passing sensitive information to and from prisoners. For months, all kinds of claims about the Muslim chaplain swirled about. There were claims that his car had been seen parked outside the home of a Muslim activist and allegations that he was having an extramarital affair. For a while his face was everywhere on television and in the American papers, but in yet another bizarre twist to the Guantanamo saga, the charges were dropped for lack of evidence. Guantanamo Bay could never be a good place for a Muslim.

"These people are giving us valuable information." Major General Geoffrey Miller sat far back in his big brown leather chair as he explained the rationale for keeping prisoners for so long without charging them with anything. "You see," he whistled through his teeth, "this is not a prison. Gitmo is an interrogation centre."

Geoffrey Miller, who was running the entire operation at Guantanamo, was from Texas and proud of it. Texas, he pointed out, was not just the home state of President Bush, but also of General Tommy Franks, who had led the invasions of both Afghanistan and Iraq. Dressed in his camouflage uniform and tightly laced black boots, he displayed that same overweening sense of "we've-got-this-right-and-don't-you-be-asking-silly-questions" as all those the Bush administration had placed in positions of power.

"These are very dangerous people, and some of them will be here for a long time," he said when I interviewed him on camera on a steep overlook above the camp. A military tribunal was about to get underway and there was talk that he was about to build an execution chamber to deal those who might be sentenced to death. While shocking, this sounded suspiciously like a tactic to encourage detainees to spill more information and to deter other potential terrorists. Though difficult for non-Americans to understand, the harsh treatment of the detainees is designed to send a message loud and clear to Osama bin Laden and his followers: you mess with us and we sure as hell will mess with you.

"In the military we plan for eventualities, but none of these plans have been approved by our senior leadership," Geoffrey Miller told me when I asked if he was making plans for possible executions.

"So you can't rule out a death chamber?"

"That's why we plan, that's why we plan," he answered, smiling broadly.

As for the dozens of suicide attempts that had been reported, a doctor on the base said that many of the detainees had been mentally unstable before they ever got there. Weeks after our visit, over twenty prisoners attempted a mass suicide by hanging, a fact that was acknowledged in the press only a year later.

That was in 2003 and the physical mistreatment of prisoners under interrogation had not yet surfaced. In the kitchen, military staff openly talked of food being used as a tool to reward or punish detainees, and Major General Miller confirmed that interrogations went on around the clock. I had noticed the camp brightly lit late into the night to prevent detainees from sleeping. But there was no hint of the nature of the allegations to come, no clue that female soldiers, women's clothing and even dogs were supposedly being used to break men whose own culture kept women firmly in their place.

AFTER THREE DAYS WE WERE ESCORTED OFF the base and back onto the plane bound for Puerto Rico, a connecting point to the US. As we waited to board, Major General Geoffrey Miller passed with his wife.

"Hi, Carole," he greeted me, impressing me that he had remembered the name of a journalist — a foreign one at that. He introduced his wife, who was going shopping in San Juan for the weekend.

The next time I heard of Major General Geoffrey Miller was when the Abu Ghraib prisoner abuse scandal surfaced. Just weeks after our visit to Camp Delta, he was sent to Iraq to make recommendations on how to extract the maximum information from detainees. It was widely reported that one of those recommendations was to use prison guards to "set the conditions" for interrogations and to soften up the detainees.

Guantanamo Bay, and since then Abu Ghraib, has inflamed anti-American feeling around the world. The isolated location, the dubious status of the prisoners, and the steady stream of mistreatment allegations has damaged the country's image perhaps more than anything else done in the name of defeating terrorism. Prisoners eventually freed without charge have claimed that they were routinely tortured with noise, beatings, sleep deprivation, extreme temperatures and cavity searches that had nothing to do with teeth. Repairing the damage could take a long time. Groups like Amnesty International claim that the tactics used at Camp Delta and in Iraq put America into the same category as some of the world's worst human right offenders. Snapshots of hooded men piled up in "naked" pyramids was something you might expect to hear about in Saddam Hussein's Iraq or in some other dark and loathsome dictatorship, not in an enlightened democracy trying to spread its values around the world.

"If they think that a few soldiers represent the entirety of America, they don't really understand America then," President Bush had responded when I had asked if he understood why the abuses at Abu Ghraib had so infuriated people. I had dealt with the American military at every level, and knew that he was right. Nowhere had I come across men and women who were so helpful, so competent and so unselfish. It was clear they were not fairly represented by the actions of Private Lynndie England from Virginia or Sergeant Charles Graner — both put on trial for their very public part in the abuses. But the idea that low-level military police had taken the hit for a system clearly out of control, while the bumbling Defense Secretary Donald Rumsfeld and senior officers such as my old acquaintance Major General Geoffrey Miller got to hide behind them was disturbing. If they didn't know about the gross acts being perpetrated on their behalf, it was their job to know. They were in charge.

ON FRIDAY, 8 JULY 2005, the rain came down in sheets in Maryland as the first of the summer's tropical storms moved swiftly through. It was the morning after the London Underground bombings and America was on high alert once again. At the train station in Baltimore, it looked as if military rule had been imposed. In the doorways leading to the train tracks, there were soldiers brandishing black machine guns — a show of strength more to ease public jitters than to deter suicide bombers. The troops did not appear to be checking people or bags and it struck me that even with their intimidating presence, anyone could still carry a ten-pound bomb on to the morning train, with little chance of detection. Sheltering from the torrential rain, the waiting passengers read their papers and were forced to consider that America's turn could come again soon. I was on my way to a mosque.

The city of Baltimore and the surrounding area is home to several thousand Muslims — mostly immigrants from Islamic countries but with some local converts too. Somewhere between three and six million Muslims live in the US — less than two per cent of the population. Baltimore's biggest mosque, the Al Rahmah, is located in a large redbrick building off a quiet road in the southern suburbs. Every Friday at lunchtime two thousand men, women and children pull into the huge parking lot and disappear inside to hear Imam Irfan Kabiruddin. After establishing that I could attend the weekly service as a guest, I was directed to the women's entrance, since the men and women pray in separate rooms. To show some respect, I had tried to dress appropriately, choosing long trousers, a headscarf and unpainted nails. Sadia, the office manager at the mosque, led me to the women's room and together we removed our shoes and sat down on a green carpet. A petite woman from Pakistan, Sadia wore designer jeans underneath her floor-length black chiffon robes.

"Excuse me while I pray," she said before launching into the bending and kneeling ritual that characterises Muslim worship. Imitating those around me, I sat in the lotus position and observed. There were women of all ages and races, Arab, Asian, African-American and a few Caucasian. I felt a hand on my shoulder and turned around to see a woman with a stud in her nose smiling at me.

"Darling," she whispered, "your back is showing."

I could not believe it: my blouse, despite my best efforts to conform, was of a length that, when I squatted, left a gap of about an inch of bare skin. I could now add it to my growing collection of outfits inappropriate for religious observances. I quickly sat up and tied a cardigan around my waist. The woman with the nose-stud nodded happily.

"A very bad act took place yesterday." A big voice suddenly filled the room. I looked around for the Imam but he was in the other section with the men; only his words reached us by loud-speaker but, judging from the tone of his voice, the news in London was important news in Baltimore too.

"We condemn this act and we clearly say that it has no place in Islam. It is against the Qur'an," he continued, pausing to let each sentence sink in.

Imam Kabiruddin was appalled by the militants and feared a new backlash against all Muslims and their faith. "What have we become — labelled as terrorists so that everywhere we go people fear us?" he asked rhetorically. "Ten or twelve years ago people would look at us with respect and awe . . . today they look at us with fear in their eyes because they are scared. If we were in their shoes, we would be scared too." The women sat in silent rows as he continued to lay bare their sorry situation. Even as an outsider, I felt uncomfortable for them. I was surrounded by people who themselves had just been attacked from within, by a minority of their own. The terrorists had not consulted them or taken their feelings into account. Watching the horror unfold on their televisions, they had been as helpless as I was; but I would not have to face the whispering and the sideways glances on the train on the way home. Apart from the certain humiliation, their religion, the very centre of their lives, was being defiled by the terrorists.

"La ilaha illa Allah, Muhammadur Rasoolu Allah," the Imam launched into Arabic. I looked over at Sadia, who explained that he was referring to the Prophet Muhammad being the true messenger of Allah. In Islam, Jesus was one of a number of prophets, as was Moses, but the most important prophet was Muhammad, who had lived fourteen hundred years ago.

"In split seconds we are destroying the name of the prophet by saying he teaches this. Nowhere will you find anything like this. He would never approve of anything like this," the Imam continued.

Though thousands of miles removed from the latest atrocity, the people in the room before him, he declared, had been assigned a new role. It would now be up to them to go out and teach non-Muslims that blowing up innocents on their way to work was not what they were about, and not what Islam was about.

By far the biggest challenge for followers of Islam has been to explain the references to *jihad* in the Qur'an. Militants interpret phrases such as "striving in the cause of Allah" as a call to arms to defend and spread Islam across the entire planet. Some verses such as this one seem to indicate that fighting will be rewarded.

"*Jihad* [holy fighting in Allah's cause] is ordained for you, though you dislike it, and it may be that you dislike a thing which is good for you and like a thing which is bad for you." Another verse in the Qur'an indicates that "it is not for a believer to kill a believer except that it be by mistake", leaving open the question of whether killing an unbeliever is condoned. In other parts of the Qur'an, killing is condemned as a serious sin.

The Imam finished with a warning that Muslims everywhere were bound by the laws of the countries they had chosen to live in and he warned against taking individual action without first discussing it with others. Militant Muslims were now hurting their brothers and the time had arrived for the majority to fight back against them. In the stiflingly hot room the congregation prayed aloud about this, and every now and then there was a roll of thunder as hundreds of pairs of knees hit the floor in unison and faces were pressed against the carpet.

Another speaker's voice then came on with a stark reminder of what Muslims now face everywhere. The Baltimore Islamic Society, the speaker announced, had run a successful campaign to free two teenage sisters from detention in New York. The sisters had been arrested because a concerned American citizen thought they fitted the mould for suicide bombers. The teenagers were both devout and had only holy pictures on their bedroom walls. "If they got away with this, the next thing they would be coming after our daughters," the voice said. One of the topics of American conversations these days is how to identify a suicide bomber, so it seemed certain that this would be the first of many such campaigns.

With everyone rushing together to leave the mosque I found it hard to keep up with Sadia. Before I found her, a robed woman approached me with a business card. It said "professional dress-maker". She had assumed that, as a newcomer, I needed some serious help with my attire. I waited around afterwards hoping for a few words with the Imam, who had managed to remain elusive. Sadia was sure he would be much too busy to meet with me but when I pointed out that the message of his sermon was that Muslims had to start talking to outsiders, she sent someone to look for him.

A few minutes later there was a knock on the door of the office attached to the mosque and Imam Kabiruddin, a huge man in long cream-coloured robes and an elaborate lace headdress beckoned me to follow him to another room. He sat behind a desk, pointed me to a seat and asked what I wanted to know. A chubby-faced boy of about eight years in a white tunic sat on a swivel chair nearby twisting and turning at speed.

"Your son?" I enquired.

"Yes," he said.

The Imam is young, maybe approaching forty. He had come to America from Bangladesh and is now a US citizen. He has a large sallow face and a mass of curly black hair. As I explained my background, he stared down at the desk in front of him, looking as if he had one dead eye. Three questions later, when I copped on that he was neither visually impaired nor shy, I just stared at the table too to spare him any further discomfort. Clearly, eye contact with a half-dressed western woman was out of the question.

But he was prepared to talk frankly. Like the militants who had attacked London, the Imam indicated that he himself was not impressed by President Bush's military involvement in Iraq and Afghanistan. But he did not agree with using violence as a tool to oppose it.

"You don't have to agree with the government of your country; you can have your own opinion, especially in America. But you voice your opinion inside the law of the land, you appeal, you write to them instead of taking things into your own hands," he said.

President Bush does not believe in talking to or even listening to disaffected Muslims hostile to the west. This approach, the Imam felt, was not helping the situation.

"Some people say that negotiations with terrorists are wrong but sometimes they have certain legitimate demands. If we don't consider those at all and we keep doing things that might add to their list, then it's going to aggravate the situation. That's what's happening today."

The terrorists' grievances were well known; they had been printed in the media too many times to mention. For two years, I had carried about a scrap of frayed newspaper in my purse containing a statement purporting to be from Al Qaeda to President Bush.

"Listen to us, you criminal, the cars of death will not stop until you concede to our demands," the statement exhorted. Top of the list of demands was that Muslim prisoners be freed from American prisons, "especially Guantanamo". The second demand was that America and its "tails" stop the war being fought against Islam and Muslims in the name of fighting terrorism.

From the statement it seemed clear that Guantanamo Bay, far from protecting against terror, had provided the terrorists with the excuse they needed to continue their killing spree. By late 2005, the Bush administration was seeking ways to send the majority of detainees back to their own countries. The Al Qaeda statement also highlighted the lingering perception among some Muslims that the war on terror was a war against Islam. The man sitting in front of me, a respected leader to thousands of American Muslims, agreed openly that issues like these were fostering resentment.

"Certain things that might happen in Iraq and Afghanistan, where Muslim children are dying because of the bombing, this will just aggravate the matter. These people . . . all they need is certain things to get sympathisers."

Though disowning the terrorists, the Imam could see that the whole situation was now entering a cycle where it was feeding off itself. "It's not a process that is going towards peace; there is no question about it," he said, both of us still looking down at the desk.

Whatever his feelings on American policy, he was still glad America was his home. Imam Kabiruddin had been to Spain and the Netherlands, where he claimed Muslims face far more serious discrimination and poverty. Even London, he believed, is a tougher place for them than anywhere in the United States.

"The people here are very good. If it was any other country where something like September 11th had taken place, Muslims would not have been able to live in that country," he said.

Imam Kabiruddin and his followers are marooned between a rock and a hard place. They crave the freedom associated with living in America, yet feel the actions the US is taking to defend itself will cause further attacks, which in turn will threaten this freedom.

The Bush administration has a different view of how to deal with terrorism. President Bush and the key neo-conservative figures in government continue to believe that freedom, brought by force if necessary, is the only sane way to defeat the ideology of the terrorists. Perhaps by reading the Al Qaeda statements addressed to him, President Bush had recognised and takes seriously the fundamentalist plan to spread Islam and Islamic law throughout the world. For better or worse, he has decided to fight this. Using America's money and its military, he has staked its reputation and its safety on an idealistic outcome. It is already coming down to a battle of wills. Al Qaeda has bet that America doesn't have the bottle or the volunteers to stay the course and will eventually refuse to take more deaths and leave the Middle East. But, true to his character, George Bush is betting that the terrorists and the insurgents will be the ones to run out of steam, fold up their tents and go home. Only time, or Allah, will tell who will prevail.

Chapter 10

Revelations

THE NAME OF A PLACE will often be enough to lure me into dropping everything and packing my bags for a journey. Never mind what's there; half the fun is in arriving at a long-dreamed-of destination and finding out if it matches my expectations. Savannah, Georgia, was one such destination that did not disappoint. With its grand houses, its ghost stories and fried green tomatoes, it oozed southern charm. Tucson, Arizona, on the other hand, failed miserably to live up to the image of a western watering-hole I had conjured up in my mind; and the feeling of uncontained anticipation that overcame me twenty-four hours from Tulsa soon dissipated on arrival in the rather bland concrete Oklahoma town.

So I was prepared for possible disappointment when I arrived in Salt Lake City, Utah, another of those places whose name had drawn me towards it with the force of a magnet. To me Utah sounds so unknowable; there's nothing in those four letters, arranged in that particular order, which evokes the slightest hint of anything familiar. Utah is mysterious, maybe even a little dark. And Salt Lake City sounds, well . . . salty.

Driving along the motorway from the airport in a rented car, I was too busy figuring out the pedals and scrutinising maps to notice anything, muttering things like "600 South" to myself as I tried to spot the exit ramp I would need to take to avoid driving round in circles for an hour. When I eventually relaxed, I felt my breath catching and heard myself uttering the immortal words "holy cow". Salt Lake City was spread out against a backdrop of jagged snow-capped peaks that seemed to hold the entire city in a huge icy embrace. The evening sun was just starting to fade and lights were flickering on across the flat expanse of buildings. Cold and mysterious to be sure — just not as I'd imagined. After arriving in so many nondescript American towns and passing through so many cluttered strips of commercial chaos, this place was jaw-droppingly beautiful. I felt as though I was driving into a paradise, a pristine city in a gleaming cloak. It is an apt setting for a place associated around the world with a religion — the Mormon Church.

These days the Mormons prefer to be known as the Church of Jesus Christ of Latter Day Saints (LDS) but they just can't shake the old nickname. It comes from the Book of Mormon, which is a text they believe was revealed specially to them by God in the 1830s. Salt Lake City is dominated by the Mormon Temple, a mystical edifice closed to everybody but worthy church members. Clustered around it is the world headquarters, housing twenty thousand church employees. Downtown Salt Lake City is also home to the Mormon Tabernacle Choir, a Mormon history museum and a massive new conference centre where the reigning Mormon leader, the Prophet, appears twice a year. Everything is big and new. Almost half the population of Salt Lake City belongs to the Mormon Church. Seven out of every ten people in the state of Utah are paid-up members. Worldwide, the Latter Day Saints claim to have twelve million members. Before coming to Utah, I had heard certain things about the Mormons — that they had several wives, that they performed ceremonies naked in the temple, that they gave all their money to the Prophet and that they all voted for George Bush. I was about to find out how much of this was true.

In a comfortable house in the southern suburb of Riverton, I met Charlotte Bartley and her neighbour Jo Leonard, both Mormons. But they were not from Utah. Two native Dubliners, they had joined the church in Ireland and England many years previously before moving here in the mid-1990s. "We were going to save up for a trip to Salt Lake City to see the Temple, but instead of coming for our holiday, we actually came over here to live," explained Charlotte, adding in her northside Dublin accent that this was all before the economic boom hit Ireland.

Jo Leonard remembered being in the Janelle Shopping Centre in Dublin the night before she left and meeting the late Jim Mitchell, the Fine Gael TD, out canvassing for votes. "'Are ya votin' for me?' he says." She wasn't. "I says to him, 'Jim, I've a passport in me pocket and I'm off to America in the morning; what can you do for me to stop me going?'" "Absolutely nothing" was Jim's candid response.

Jo is a born storyteller and after just a few minutes I felt as if I had lived next door to her all my life. Both she and Charlotte looked remarkably youthful for grandmothers and I could just picture them both trying on the latest fashions at the Janelle Shopping Centre. Instead, we were five thousand miles away talking about religion.

Jo, who was originally from Cabra, first heard about the Mormons as a teenager while talking to a friend across the garden fence. "She told me about these two gorgeous-looking American fellas going round the estates. The only problem was they didn't drink or smoke or date!" Worse again, they had lured the friend's sister into joining the Mormons, prompting a family crisis. There was some good news, however. The sister's husband, who up to then had happily drunk eight pints a night and smoked like a trooper, had given the whole lot up at the request of the church. "That got my attention," said Jo, explaining that her own family was puffing away several packets of cigarettes a day between them, even after their mother had died of cancer. Curiosity got the better of her and she went along to listen to the Americans. They were handsome alright but she remembers being attracted by something else. Jo, a Catholic, liked the fact that they claimed to be led by a prophet, a human messenger from God himself.

Joseph Smith was the first Mormon prophet and the founder of the religion. His followers believe that in 1829, as a young man living in upstate New York, Smith was called to "restore" the gospel of Jesus Christ. This calling occurred in the woods at the back of Smith's home where he claimed to have seen "two personages whose brightness and glory defy all description standing above me in the air . . . One of them spake unto me, calling me by my name and said, pointing to the other, 'This is my beloved son. Hear him.'" There were more apparitions, including one from an angel called Moroni, who said that a book was hidden in a hill and that on its gold-plated pages Smith would find the everlasting gospel. After some fruitless searches, Smith eventually retrieved the book and in a sustained burst of divine inspiration translated it from a language he had never even heard of before then. This supernatural translation became known as the Book of Mormon. Today, it is regarded by the Latter Day Saints as a third testament, to be read in conjunction with the Bible. During his life, Smith allegedly received many other revelations, including one which he insisted was a direct order from God. He said he was told to take as many wives as possible.

"I felt it was important to have revelations." Jo tried to convey what it was that had encouraged her to look beyond the Catholic faith she was reared on in Cabra.

Charlotte Bartley from Artane was sipping on a glass of iced water listening as Jo talked. The Mormon rule against caffeine meant there was no cup of tea on offer in this Irish home, though the smell of hot baking bread wafted in from the kitchen all evening. Charlotte was blonde and trim and I remarked on how well she looked for a grandmother. "It's the reels," she explained, telling me about her involvement with an Irish dancing group in Salt Lake City. Irish dancing is considered a good wholesome social outlet for Mormon children. The group is mainly American but there is a small contingent from Cork and Dublin, all Mormons.

Charlotte's husband Roddy was eating his dinner in the corner but had an ear on our conversation. He had encountered the Mormons when he and Charlotte were living in England. She was not happy about it but ended up attending one of their talks, en route to a wedding one weekend. According to Charlotte, she only went along so she could drag Roddy out of there in time for the wedding. But that's not what happened. "I went into that house and I can only say there was a special feeling in it," she said, looking upwards as she attempted to describe what it was that stopped her in her tracks and led her to a religion she had regarded with deep suspicion. "To this day I can only say that it had to be something from above, divine intervention if you want to call it that, but whatever it was I couldn't deny it." They stayed for hours listening to the missionaries and never did make it to the wedding that night.

In the meantime, Jo had herself become a Mormon and met Tony, a working-class Dubliner who had heard about them in a pub. After a civil marriage in Dublin, they married in the Mormon temple in Surrey. Unlike in the US, the Irish government does not recognise a temple marriage. Mormon marriage, I discovered, is also for the long haul. When a couple weds in a temple, they are not just joined together in holy matrimony until death do them part. They are "sealed" to their spouse "for time and all eternity". This, they believe, ensures that they will still be married in the next life. Mormons routinely perform ceremonies to "seal" themselves to their parents and their children to them, believing that this will keep them all together in the afterlife.

"I loved the idea of eternal marriage," Charlotte smiled over at Roddy, who was busily scoffing the last of his dinner. "I thought I could have more than one wife," he snapped back, before planting a kiss on her cheek and disappearing out the front door. After joining the church and going through a temple marriage, Roddy and Charlotte had baptised their own three children as Mormons, a ritual that can be performed by a family member or by a priest.

Jo is intensely proud that her husband is a priest. "Tony just wears a shirt and tie and goes to work to earn a living but if I need a blessing, my husband holds the priesthood." Anyone over the age of twelve can be considered for the priesthood, as long as they are deemed to be worthy church members and are well versed in Mormon doctrine.

ONE OF THE MOST CONTROVERSIAL ASPECTS of the mainstream Mormon faith is the practice of baptising the dead. Devout Mormons are obliged to trace their ancestors as far back as possible and to baptise them retrospectively in a temple ceremony. The seriousness they attach to this was evident at the Mormon genealogy library downtown. Established in 1894 to help church members identify their forbears, today it houses the records of three billion people who lived and died over the past three centuries. With legal permission, the library has filmed records of births, deaths and marriages from all over the world. These are stored on two and a half million rolls of microfilm. In case the library might be destroyed in a fire or terrorist attack, copies of everything are held in a vault in the Wasatch Mountains that surround the city. The vault has been earthquake-proofed at a cost of several million dollars.

Vona Williams, an unassuming middle-aged woman, took me through the huge library. On floor after floor, hundreds of people, mainly elderly retirees, were bent over microfilm, all busily searching for someone to baptise. On an upper floor, the British Isles section was a hive of hushed activity. The first thing I saw was a poster about Ellis Island, where hundreds of thousands of Irish had entered America. Vona confirmed that they had the records from there too. As we tiptoed around, she produced a reference index from my home county of Leitrim. "A lot of people of English and Irish ancestry have been baptised by the church," she told me as she leafed through the book. As the pages turned, I spotted local place-names like Aughnasheelin, Bornacoola and Fenagh. I had never thought I would locate my own family so far from home in a Mormon repository, so I was barely paying attention when Vona asked for my grandfather's name and approximate date of birth and went searching. Minutes later, she was back with a small white box containing the microfilm of births registered in the parish of Kiltoghert in 1907. Threading the microfilm around the sprockets on the projector, I spooled through looking for any sign of a Kevin Doherty. As familiar last names and townlands spun past, I was getting nervous that I would find him, and then suddenly — there was no denying it — there he was: old Kevin Patrick Doherty, born 29 May 1907 to parents Michael Doherty and Susan Purcell, my great-grandparents. I knew that several of my ancestors had come to make their lives in America and they could well have Mormon descendants now trying to baptise everyone in the family. A Catholic all his life, my grandfather from Carrick-on-Shannon could easily be rebaptised by a group he most likely had never heard of. In fact, it was becoming clear that, one day, we could all be saved by the Mormons.

Ireland, Vona explained, had not been as forthcoming with its records as other countries. The Irish bishops, she indicated, were a bit reluctant to hand over information that could mark out Irish people for baptism and many of the most useful records had been destroyed in a fire in Dublin during the Civil War. But they did have one recent stroke of luck with Ireland when they got their hands on a "super index" of wills going all the way back to 1740. Vona became excited as she showed me the section now housing the wills of Ireland's sons and daughters.

"What about all those who lived prior to the 1700s?" I asked, anxious to know how far back this wholesale harvesting of the deceased extended. Identifying these ancestors, she confirmed, was a major headache without records, but she was optimistic that help would soon be arriving — from above.

"We hope the lost ones will show up some day," she said wistfully. "It's our belief that when Christ comes again there will be a thousand years of peace on earth where he will be ruler and, during that time, we will solve a lot of the problems we can't solve now because the people will be right there."

Far from stealing souls, the Mormons believe they are doing a service to the dead. Dan Witherspoon, a Mormon who has performed these baptisms, explained that it is simply about extending an opportunity to those who have never heard the gospel — the Book of Mormon — to be saved. Performing the proxy baptism, he stressed, is just one half of the job. It is up to the deceased person on the other side to accept or reject the offer. "It's not like we are forcing them to become Mormons. We are giving them a blank cheque and they can cash it or not," he said. Witherspoon, the editor of *Sunstone*, a Mormon news magazine, considers himself a liberal member of the faith and yet has no problem with the baptisms. But relatives of Jewish Holocaust victims have strongly objected to the practice. Given that the victims had died because they were Jewish, their relatives are furious that another group is now performing secret ceremonies on their behalf.

For Dan Witherspoon, it's all about fulfilling the obligations of his faith. As we chatted in a hotel lobby, he pointed out his white all-in-one undergarment, which he wears constantly to remind him of his duties as a Latter Day Saint.

With all this information coming at me, I had forgotten to enquire at the genealogy library if my grandfather, Kevin Doherty, had actually been baptised by proxy, so I e-mailed Vona to find out. I suspect he himself would be greatly amused. I can just hear him saying, "I don't care what they do, they can have me." Two days later, she replied. He was not on the list of the redeemed. No direct descendants had claimed him. However, one hundred and twenty other Dohertys born in the same area had been baptised by the Mormons, including a Kevin Doherty born in 1750. So it was true after all — the Dohertys of Leitrim had indeed been readied for the Eternal Kingdom.

TOM BRIGHTON HAD JUST RETURNED to Salt Lake City from Ireland after completing a three-year stint as head of the Mormon mission there. "We have a house in Castleknock," he told me when I met him on the sixth floor of the Latter Day Saints headquarters downtown. Tom, a tall thin man in his sixties, has a mild manner and a warm smile. You get the feeling he knows his place in the grand scheme of Mormon hierarchy and knows it is a humble place. He and his wife had just built their dream home on the side of a mountain in Woodland Hills, Utah, when the call came to go to Ireland. He had already devoted much of his life to the church, but felt he should go. The church expected him and his wife to sell their new home but he put his foot down on that one. There were other sacrifices associated with his Irish posting. Because the church forbids mission leaders to leave their posts, even for a few days, he could not attend his own son's wedding back in the US. Far from seeming bitter, I got the sense from Tom that when God's work calls, it is a privilege to miss your son's wedding.

The church in Ireland, he explained, has three dioceses: one in Finglas run by a local farmer; another in Northern Ireland which is looked after by a retired prison officer; and a third in Limerick. The LDS owns or runs almost twenty buildings across the country and has over eight thousand people on its membership rolls, though not all of these are currently practising. "It's not easy at all," Tom laughed loudly when I ask how he could manage to grab the attention of Irish people for anything spiritual these days. Immigrants such as Africans, Eastern Europeans, Chinese and expats from the US, he agreed, were more enthusiastic. Trying to get people to listen to a talk about the prophets was a challenge, but the concept of eternal marriage always sparked interest. The Irish, he felt, still had common misconceptions about the Mormon church. "They think we are Jehovah's Witnesses and that polygamy is still allowed; and they think we are paid and that somehow there is a financial motivation in this," he said.

Although Mormon missionaries have been coming to Ireland since Jo Leonard first met the gorgeous-looking American fellas back in Cabra, the church did not achieve any official recognition until recently.

"We will be there for the long term," believed Tom, explaining that he had hired a solicitor to go through the process of officially registering the church. He smiled to himself. "I am the founder of the Church in Ireland," he joked, noting that he had to put his name on the official application to the government. At any one time, according to Tom, there are several missionaries operating around the country. There is even a stake (a small local division) in Sligo, which meets in a small back room in the town. It holds about twelve people.

Tom was perturbed by the pervasive drinking culture and the drug abuse he had encountered in Dublin and felt the Mormons had something to say on family values. "We have a voice I think the government will value," he said. Mormons in Ireland who want to marry in a temple or perform baptisms are still travelling to England. According to Tom, they have an arrangement with the high-speed ferry which takes church members over and back once a month for just eighteen euro. "They are down at the ferry at six o'clock in the morning and come back at ten at night."

"Any sign of the church building a temple in Ireland?" I asked.

"Maybe some day," he replied.

AT THE RIPE OLD AGE OF NINETY-FIVE, Gordon B. Hinckley was still running the Mormon empire when I visited Salt Lake City. He had been selected to lead the church after the death of Howard Hunter in 1995 at the age of eighty-seven. Each new prophet is considered a successor to the Mormon founder Joseph Smith and, as well as expanding the church, he is also a "seer" who, it is widely accepted, receives revelations from God. After years of negative publicity for the Saints, prophet Hinckley had engaged the American media and, unlike his predecessors, he had dropped any pretence of having access to an open hotline to God. "He has backed away from any claim of meeting God face to face," claimed Dan Witherspoon. "He feels he is led by the still, small voice inside, not by thunder and lightning. There has been no whiz-bang revelation in half a century."

For a Mormon, meeting Hinckley is like meeting the Pope. Nobody I met around Temple Square, in the genealogy library or in the church museum had ever had the privilege of meeting him but the Dubliners had got close. Several years ago on a visit to Ireland, Gordon B. Hinckley had visited Jo Leonard's mother-in-law in hospital. "That was when he was one of the Twelve Apostles," said Jo, referring to the elite group from which the next prophet emerges. She had bumped into another of the Twelve doing his washing at the mission house in Dublin. "He was just as sacred to me standing in the laundry room as he would be in the temple," she said, recalling her brief encounter.

Over at the Mormon history museum, it was clear that this was still a very young religion — barely one hundred and seventy years old. Among the exhibits were copies of the plans for the very first temple, apparently dictated by a revelation from above. Even the gun used to murder Joseph Smith in a prison shootout was there. (In 1844, Smith had been arrested following the destruction of a newspaper that had been critical of him. He was subsequently charged with treason. An angry mob had stormed the prison where he had been held, and Smith had been shot and killed.)

What I could not find was any reference to the issue that had dogged the church since its inception — polygamy.

"Excuse me." I approached one of the church employees who were keeping a close watch on visitors. "Why is there nothing about polygamy here?"

"Oh, it's over here," the woman pointed to a wall display where a single line of text was devoted to the subject.

"Is that it?"

"I suppose it's just too controversial," she replied in a whisper, confirming my suspicions that the Saints have taken it upon themselves to rewrite history. They had done so despite the fact that tens of thousands of Americans who claim to be Mormons are still living the principle of plural marriage. Many of them, members of the Fundamentalist Mormon church (FLDS), are located in a place called Colorado City, on the border between Utah and Arizona.

THERE WAS ONLY ONE WAY TO GET THERE in the time I had available and, as luck would have it, that meant getting on a small turbo-prop plane. Aside from the extra turbulence as it ascended out of Salt Lake City on a Sunday morning, there was a cacophonous screeching of the engines. Luckily, the sky was cloudless and the scenery so distracting that I had soon forgotten my nerves. Behind the snow-capped mountains of the city was what I presumed to be the salt lake, appearing like a huge flat strand at low tide. Beyond this we bounced above hills that were more redolent of a Tuscan scene — and then everything turned orange and red and rocky. We descended towards a narrow ledge which served as the airstrip at St George in southern Utah. I closed my eyes, clenched my fists and sweated. In minutes we were deposited safely on the ledge.

After this, hiring a car and setting off for a new location was relaxing. From a slow reluctant start several months earlier, I had got used to driving in America. I had progressed from quiet roads to six-lane highways, wondering why I had put it off for so long. I had yet to be ticketed or towed and had avoided any accidents. Getting out on the open road in a brand new rental car was now something to relish rather than to fear. I still panicked on occasions when I had to stop for gas and couldn't for the life of me figure out how to open the tank!

For weeks I had been looking at Colorado City as a tiny speck on the map between Utah and Arizona, and practically salivating about getting there. Judging by how far off the beaten track it is, I had already printed up a set of mental pictures. I imagined dusty desert highways and a heat haze, the type you see in front of you as you drive along a tar road in one hundred degree weather. This time, I was almost spot on. But the landscape was even more dramatic than I had imagined. Once out of St George, a city of terracotta villas, the roads wound in and out between red rock mountains. There was little in the way of housing or humanity. Every now and then I passed a cluster of mobile homes which looked as if they had been dropped into the middle of a field in no particular order. The temperature rose steadily and, wouldn't you know it, after several minutes of twiddling knobs I could still only get the air vents to spew out more heat into my face. The desert, I decided, was not the place for a woman travelling alone to ask strangers for help, so I drove on with the windows down.

For forty miles I drove through uninhabited wilderness until, seemingly out of nowhere, a large town materialised in the distance.

Mirage?

Nope.

Hilldale is the very last town in the state of Utah at this point on the border, and Colorado City, next door, is the first one in Arizona. In reality they are the one town, but because of differences in how they use daylight saving time, an hour is gained by crossing the border. I leave the top of Hilldale at eleven o'clock and reach the bottom of Colorado City at a minute past noon.

Hilldale and Colorado City used to be known jointly as Short Creek when the fundamentalists came to settle here in the 1920s. But about twenty years ago they changed the name in an effort to banish memories of the Short Creek raid. The raid took place in 1953 when the state forcibly removed hundreds of women and children in a crackdown on polygamy. Local sympathy for the fundamentalists turned the episode into a public relations disaster and the women and children were eventually returned to their husbands. Before coming here, I had read that, in 2003, the families affected had erected a monument commemorating the fiftieth anniversary of the Short Creek raid. But half an hour later, Warren Jeffs, the local fundamentalist leader, had ordered it removed. As punishment, he expelled several male community members from Colorado City and reassigned their wives and children to other men. The monument had been erected without his permission and would have been sure to draw outside interest.

The first thing I noticed was that the homes in Colorado City were all bigger than normal. Not only that, they seemed to have their backs to the main road as if to say to passers-by that they wanted to be left alone. The houses were basic and functional, mainly clapboard, but the ones that you could see behind the tall fences were large enough to have ten or fifteen rooms. Unlike the Amish community in Pennsylvania, there was no visitors' centre or museum. Out there in the desert there was nothing to indicate that this is home to ten thousand Mormon fundamentalists who believe, like Joseph Smith did, that God has commanded them to practise the principle of plural marriage or polygamy.

The mainstream Mormons, to which Jo and Charlotte belong, had banned polygamy in 1890 after pressure from the government to obey the law of the land, but the fundamentalists believe that living "the principle" is their only way to heaven. They shun publicity and are under strict orders from their leaders to refuse all contact with strangers.

Looking from the road, I could not see a single sign of life around the houses — not even a dog. Eventually a mini-van with darkened windows passed and I could make out the heads of several children and adults inside. Against all the advice I had received before coming, I followed the van around the back of the town, past numerous compounds, and finally found myself in front of a huge white building. There were several hundred cars already parked outside it and scores of others were just arriving. The building, which was the size of a large sports complex, was bustling with people coming and going from every side. Because it was Sunday, I assumed this could only be a religious service of some kind and from what I was seeing those going to it were strict adherents to "the principle".

I saw men dressed formally in dark suits enter the building followed by groups of women. The women walked behind the men and all of them were carrying small babies and ushering toddlers and older children ahead of them. I parked a short distance away from the church and watched as the families arrived. Some men were accompanied by two women, others by three or four. In all cases the women looked to be in their late teens or early twenties, dressed uniformly in ankle-length one-piece dresses, their hair drawn back in a bun or a plait. They came in mini-vans and even small buses. As they passed my car, I was on the receiving end of several stares, but nobody came near me. I pretended to be studying a map, but I am sure they knew I was not lost. A white limousine pulled up and dropped off another large family of about twelve. I spotted one young woman being followed by three men and thought to myself that there may some justice in this after all! For over an hour the parade into the church continued until there was no place left to park. Vans then just parked on the road and on the grass verge. I have no idea how many people were inside, but it must have been several thousand.

Colorado City is a very young city; according to the official town statistics, the average age is just fourteen. "By the time you are fourteen you are focused on getting married," Brooke Adams, an American journalist who has observed the fundamentalists, told me. In some cases, young girls are even married off to their fathers or uncles. She believes there are between thirty thousand and fifty thousand Mormon fundamentalists in Utah and, with high birth rates, their numbers are still growing.

Not all families practise polygamy. A small number of young men and women have run away from Colorado City to avoid it, but most just go along with the lifestyle, perhaps because of religious fervour or fear or because they don't know any other way of life.

Unlike other groups who choose a different lifestyle, such as the Amish, children in this community are not automatically given the option to leave. Since the botched Short Creek raid, the authorities have turned a blind eye to the situation and are just now starting to crack down again, but proving polygamy or the sexual abuse of minors is difficult. "Few witnesses will come forward to testify against their own families," Brooke Adams explained, adding that the men legally marry just one woman and take the rest as "spiritual wives". Some of the community leaders are rumoured to have as many as twenty of these and nobody can say that they are breaking the law. Two out of three residents of Colorado City are on state welfare, but again, without witnesses, it is difficult to prove any wrongdoing. Fundamentalist Mormons take pride in working the government to their financial advantage, an activity they call "bleeding the beast". In 2005 the Utah Attorney General launched a renewed effort to prosecute for alleged polygamy, incest and welfare fraud and offered support to group members willing to come forward.

I drove on past the church towards Canaan, the cliff-like rock that is a backdrop to the town. A car appeared in my rear-view mirror but I ignored it. Closer to the mountain I came to a dead end. It was clear that the car had followed me. I was in the middle of nowhere and had probably attracted too much attention, hanging around the church for over two hours. There are times, as a journalist, when you know you should have heeded the advice you were given and stayed out of trouble. I felt my heart pounding as the car drew up directly behind me. As far I could tell, I was not legally trespassing, so, as I waited for the inevitable confrontation, I mentally rehearsed a little speech about freedom and liberty and my right to drive on the public road. Imagine my relief when I saw a stooped woman of about eighty in a long pink dress getting out of the car behind me. With her was a boy of about four, also stooped, and both were carrying empty water cans. She said nothing and didn't even glance in my direction as she passed.

"Is there fresh water here?" I asked.

"Yes, just up here," she said, pointing towards Canaan.

She smiled at me, I smiled at the kid and my pulse returned to normal.

THINGS HAD REPORTEDLY BEEN getting nasty in Colorado City since Warren Jeffs took over the United Effort Plan (UEP) from his ninety-something-year-old father Rulon Jeffs. The UEP is one of the largest branches of the fundamentalist Mormons and you see the letters on the side of buildings like you might see "UVF" or "IRA" in Belfast. What little reporting there is from here suggests disagreements over his more autocratic style of leadership, splits and expulsions. The latest word was that Jeffs, a painfully thin-looking man in his fifties, had left Colorado City and moved his family to a new compound in El Dorado, Texas.

"We were glad they didn't all kill themselves on 6 April," Dan Witherspoon had told me back in Salt Lake City. Jeffs had predicted that the world would end on 6 April 2005. "They had been building a huge temple on their property in El Dorado and were rushing to finish it. There was concern he would do a Jim Jones," he said.

Setting themselves against the mainstream in America, the fundamentalists run their own private schools and their own businesses. They are hard workers according to Brooke Adams and, aside from the issues that draw unwanted attention to these people, they live isolated lives. There were no satellite dishes or TV antennas on any of the houses. Like other fundamentalist groups I had met, they felt the need to protect themselves from their own country.

I did not get to ask anyone whom they had voted for or if they had voted at all, but Utah is staunch Bush country. Over seventy per cent of voters supported the President in 2004, the highest percentage of any of the fifty states. Utah, which has a history of rebelling against the government over issues relating to the Mormon faith, is now one of the most patriotic states in America, sending many of its sons and daughters off to war. But election exit polls consistently show that married people also tend to vote Republican, and they sure are married here — sealed for time and all eternity.

As I drove back out of Colorado City, a man changing the tyre on his truck was being closely watched by five of his young children. Observing them, it was obvious they had seen nothing more exciting all week — a picture of simplicity in a very complicated place.

AFTER EVERYTHING I HAD SEEN, Jo and Charlotte back in Salt Lake City appeared very normal. They told me that they still attracted a few strange looks any time they go home to Dublin, especially at Catholic funerals and weddings, but it doesn't stop them attending. "I still go to the Pro Cathedral or St Michan's," said Charlotte, "but I don't have any regrets about where I am and why I am here." And Jo told me her family attended Mormon services with her when they came to Salt Lake City. "It's not all that different from what Mammy taught us," she claimed. As I left Utah, it seemed to me that everyone I had met was looking for the same happy ending and that the different paths they were taking didn't matter so much as how they travelled those paths. For some, it involved a rejection of the modern world; for others it meant going without the cup of tea; and at least for some it meant baptising the deceased Dohertys of Leitrim. Perhaps that dark unknowable place I started out from did unmask something for me after all.

Chapter 11

The Catholic Jew

*T*HERE IS AN OLD BELFAST JOKE that you have probably heard. A Belfast man asks a guy in a bar: "Are you a Catholic or a Protestant?" "I'm a Jew," the man replies. "Yeah, sure, I know you're a Jew," says the Belfast man, "but are you a Catholic Jew or a Protestant Jew?"

Jhon Berenstein was the name of my great-great-grandfather. He was born and lived in Riga, the capital of Latvia. Family records suggest that Jhon Berenstein and his family left Riga for London in the nineteenth century and that in 1859 he married Jewish girl Sarah Franks in the Great Synagogue in Brick Lane. I had heard all about my great-great-grandparents long before coming to America, but what I did not know was that, because Jewish heritage passes through the female line, all descendants on the maternal side are considered members of the Jewish faith, including me and my three siblings. So although Sarah's daughter, my great-grandmother Caroline, became a Protestant in London and my grandmother Rebecca converted from the Protestant faith to

Roman Catholicism, I would still be considered by some to be one hundred per cent Jewish.

This fact was disclosed to me by an Orthodox Jew whom I met at the bar of the Wayfarer Hotel in Manchester, New Hampshire, during the 2004 presidential election primaries. Despite my earnest protestations that decades of mass attendance, confirmation by a bishop and heaps of Roman Catholic guilt had knocked it out of me, I was, he insisted, given a Jewish name at Mount Sinai. And while he claimed that religious Jews do not try to convert others, he happily announced that, in my case, there was no need. I was already in the door of the synagogue and could even marry a Jew without changing a thing, if the fancy took me. This was all earth-shaking news, in part because of the controversial nature and history of my new identity, but mainly because I had come face-to-face with my own ignorance. Growing up in the Ireland of the 1970s and 1980s, I had sat through countless religion classes, had memorised parts of the Bible and, as a live-in pupil at a Mercy convent, had attended mass every morning, generally before sunrise, for five years. Together with my fellow boarders at the convent in Newtownforbes in County Longford, I had recited the Rosary almost daily, keeping all fifteen Mysteries on the tip of my tongue as I waited for the inevitable tap on the shoulder.

"Please give out the Sorrowful Mysteries."

"Yes, Sister."

Sometimes we were so nervous, we would manage to recall the Mysteries, only to forget the words of the Hail Mary! When a girl lost her beads, we would break up the available sets, wrapping the truncated sections tightly around our hands to avoid a telling-off. We were very religious. What I don't recall is learning anything about any other religions or value systems. Not that there was anything wrong with Roman Catholicism, but it would have been helpful to have had enough information about other faiths to be able to work out that I had Jewish blood.

"WHAT DO YOU WANT ME TO TELL YOU? You are a Jew." Rabbi Nochum Light confirmed the religious diagnosis when I met him in my newly adopted home town of Annapolis in Maryland a year later.

"Have I abandoned my faith, then?" I asked, explaining that I was quite happy to be a Roman Catholic.

"You have not abandoned it. You didn't know; it's a different category. It's not like you knew it and left. Now it's a good thing that you are going to learn about it." We met at the Aleph Bet day school for Jewish children, which over the phone sounded to me like the Alice Betts school. I discovered its proper name only when the taxi driver deposited me at the front door and no one there had ever heard of Alice Betts.

My next *faux pas* was trying to shake hands with Rabbi Light, a business-like man of average height with jet black hair and beard and piercing blue eyes. As I extended my hand, he drew back and, looking rather embarrassed, beckoned his wife Hindy to come and greet me formally. Hours later, after we had talked, he explained that for Orthodox Jews handshakes are a sign of affection reserved for good friends and family only. He may have been trying to soften the blow for me; I later heard that the real reason was probably that Orthodox men do not touch other women.

The Lights, both still in their mid-twenties, had recently arrived in Annapolis from New York to raise a family and start a religious community called a Chabad house. Their primary interest was in meeting and ministering to unaffiliated Jews who were no longer practising their faith, and people like me who never even knew they were Jewish. Just over fifty per cent of America's Jews subscribe to Judaism, and surveys have shown that less than one-fifth of Jews regularly attend a synagogue.

BECAUSE I WAS SO BEREFT of basic knowledge, I decided that the best place for me to learn about my newly discovered heritage was among a group of five- and six-year-olds. It was April, just before Passover, and my first lesson was in how to make Matzah.

"What are we going to make today?" Rabbi Light enquired of the twenty-four kids and one conspicuous adult sitting on the floor of the school gym in front of him. "Matzah," we shouted. The Rabbi's baby son Mendel laughed hysterically at us from his stroller parked at the top of the class. During Passover (Pesach, in Hebrew) observant Jews eat only that food which is Kosher or suitable for the feast. Bread, because it is made from leavened dough, is not considered kosher and is replaced by Matzah — flour and water baked quickly before it rises. Matzah has the consistency and taste of a stale diet cracker.

"How fast must we make it?" asked the Rabbi, furiously mixing the dough in a bowl. After much prompting, a kindergarten girl provided the answer that every Jew should know: "Eighteen minutes."

"Yes, if it takes more than eighteen minutes, the dough starts to rise and if it does it becomes bread," said the Rabbi. The Jewish feast of Passover commemorates the deliverance of the Jews from slavery in Egypt over three thousand years ago — the Exodus. They fled from Egypt so quickly, they didn't have time to let their bread rise and had to make do with unleavened bread or Matzah. Passover itself comes from the angel of death "passing over" or sparing Jewish homes when he killed all the first-born sons of Egypt. Jews were asked to slay a lamb, leaving its blood on the doorposts so the angel would know which houses to avoid.

By now, we had been given rolling pins and a chunk of the newly mixed dough. Even though my family have been in the bakery business for over a century, my dough stuck stubbornly to the pin. "Use more flour," the rabbi suggested, urging me to get a move on or I would end up with useless bread. The dough had to be rolled paper thin and punctured, all before being rushed to the portable oven which Hindy Light had brought with her from home.

Unlike the Lights, most of the children around me were not Orthodox Jews. Some of them were the less strict Conservative Jews and the rest were Reform Jews, who are even more relaxed in the practice of the faith. Yet all were planning to observe the basic rules of Passover, which I discovered were pretty complicated and time-consuming. Following the rules of the Torah, every Jewish person must clean their homes of any trace of bread or "leavened" products before celebrating Passover. This means that crumbs stuck anywhere in the kitchen, even under the fridge, have to be cleaned out. The offending matter is known as "Chametz" (pronounced "ham-ets"). The weekly bulletin which I picked up from the synagogue beside the Aleph Bet school suggested searching for Chametz the night before Passover with a lighted candle in one hand and a brush in the other while reciting the following prayer: "Bo-ruch Ah-toh Ha-shem Elo-ky-nu Me-lech Hah-o-lom Ah-sher kih-dih-sha-nu Bih-mitz-vo-tov Vih-tzi-vah-nu al Be-or Chametz", which roughly translates as "God help me find the breadcrumbs".

All kitchen utensils used to make bread or cakes are to be sold or placed symbolically in the ownership of a non-Jew. The rabbi usually offers to effect the transaction, which on this occasion had to be completed before the twelfth day of Nisan 5765, that being 21 April 2005. On top of this there are rules for washing the pots and pans that will be used to make the Passover meal. Sinks and ovens must be thoroughly cleaned and glassware is supposed to be soaked for three days, changing the water every twenty-four hours. After discovering all this, the Catholic requirement of fasting for an hour before mass on Sunday, or the largely ignored tradition of fish on Friday, did not seem like much to ask!

As our piping hot Matzah came out of the makeshift oven in the gym, Rabbi Light declared that it was no good for Passover, since it had taken us all more than eighteen minutes to make it. We ate it right there, but glue would have tasted better. For the school's mock Passover Seder the following day, there would be factory-produced Matzah.

As we gathered up the tainted utensils that would now have to be scrubbed and possibly sold, I asked the Rabbi why the rules were so detailed.

"We try to do it the same way our ancestors did," he said, referring to their hasty departure from Egypt three millennia ago. "We live it," he added. Were it not for the Exodus, the Rabbi believed the Jews might still be slaving away somewhere along the Nile and would never have received the Torah from Moses. It followed, he said, that the waters of the Red Sea would never have been parted and God would never have given the Jews the nation of Israel.

THIS QUEST TO LEARN MORE about America's Jews also took me to New York, specifically to the diamond district off Fifth Avenue. Here, shop after shop is crammed with gold, silver and gems. If everyone in New York purchased something, you can bet they still wouldn't manage to empty these shops. Inside, the keepers of the gleaming treasures stand ready to make a sales pitch or adjust a watch or ring to fit a customer's needs — anything to move the merchandise out the door. The entire trade is run by Hasidic Jews, one of the strictest branches of Judaism in the US. In the evening, I watched them leave, dressed in black coats and fedoras, with their long ringlets or *payot* bobbing as they hurried on to buses or disappeared into the subways and trains that would take them home to New Jersey or Brooklyn. On a Saturday afternoon I took the train from Manhattan, getting off at a stop that I thought was close to Williamsburg, a big Jewish neighbourhood in Brooklyn. After establishing that I was still miles away, I jumped into a taxi.

"Lee Avenue, please," I said to the driver.

"Are you meeting someone there?" He was looking at me in his rear-view mirror and thinking that I must be mistaken with the address. He had a long beard, but since it was the Sabbath I had to assume that he wasn't Jewish or he wouldn't be out driving a cab.

"No, just going for a look," I told him.

He examined me again in the mirror. As usual, I was underdressed for my assignment. It was ninety degrees out and I was wearing a short skirt and a sleeveless top.

"They are good people," he said, referring to the Hasidic Jews. He was a Muslim from Afghanistan and, from what he was telling me, he had more in common with the Orthodox Jews than with anyone else in Brooklyn.

"You lose your children in Christian neighbourhoods," he said, sounding as though he was starting on a cab driver's rant.

"What do you mean?" I asked.

"You lose them to gays and drugs."

ON LEE AVENUE THE SHOPS WERE SHUT and the streets silent. There was no traffic. On the Jewish Sabbath, from sundown on Friday until Saturday evening, strictly observant Jews won't drive cars or handle electrical appliances. If the refrigerator breaks down, they have to wait until Sunday to fix it. If they need a light turned on, they must ask a gentile to flip the switch. The few people who were out and about were men, all dressed in long black silk jackets tied at the waist like bathrobes. Some of the younger men wore yarmulkes or skull caps and others had fedoras, while some sported huge round hats that looked like fur doughnuts on top of their heads.

More than at any other time I had gone to observe a fundamentalist group, I felt that I stuck out like a sore thumb on Lee Avenue. One young man enquired if I was lost but refused to answer follow-up questions. Most of the men looked at the ground as I passed them, intent on avoiding eye contact. I'm sure it was the state of undress thing again.

"What do you do all day Saturday?" I had asked the Orthodox Jew at the bar in New Hampshire who had filled me in on the implications of my Jewish ancestry. "We study the Torah," he said. One of the key things I learned that distinguishes my Jewish heritage from my Christian heritage is how the Bible is read. Christians read both the Old and New Testaments. Jews read only the Old Testament. Christians believe that Jesus came and died on the cross for all sinners and that he will come again, as foretold in the Book of Revelations. Jews regard Jesus as just another historical figure. They are still waiting for the Messiah, believing that he has not shown up at all yet. When he does come, they believe he will rebuild Solomon's Temple and that his arrival will signal the start of an era of peace and prosperity on earth. Most Orthodox Jews also subscribe to Kabbalah, a Jewish mysticism they believe to be capable of giving them a secret knowledge of God.

It's not hard to spot an Orthodox Jew, but they are in a minority among the Jews in America. Most Jewish people I met there were from the Conservative and Reform branches of Judaism. For two years, I had shared an office with Stephanie, a Conservative Jew and the granddaughter of a Holocaust survivor who came to Canada from Eastern Europe. In Stephanie's home, Jewish traditions are regularly observed. Friday nights are generally reserved for a family dinner, where the wine and Challah bread are ritually blessed. Traditional matzahball soup, a thin chicken broth with meal dumplings, is served along with delicious beef brisket. Her young son was circumcised after birth and he will have a Bar Mitzvah on reaching the age of thirteen, while his sister will have a Bat Mitzvah when she reaches twelve.

Other acquaintances describe themselves as "cultural Jews" — those who claim not to be religious but who like to keep some of the traditions, such as marrying into the faith and laying on vast spreads of food for the family on Jewish feast days. Then there is the stand-up comic Jew, such as Woody Allen or Jackie Mason, who tends to gently mock his heritage by turning it into a continuous comedy. This self-deprecation, so common among American Jews, has historical roots in anti-Semitism, leading them to make fun of themselves before others do.

At the office, I picked up some of the Jewish lexicon from Stephanie; instead of carrying stuff around, I was *schlepping* it, and the man in the next apartment was no longer an idiot but a downright *schmuck!*

BUT THIS IS JUST ONE SIDE of the Jewish coin in America. The other side is Zionism, a very different matter. Not all Jews are Zionists and some non-Jews are. Zionism began as a political movement to establish a national homeland for Jews in Palestine, the location of the ancient kingdom of Israel. Since the birth of the modern state of Israel in 1948, Zionism has been about protecting and developing Israel and encouraging Jews to settle there. In America this goes beyond religion. It is about politics and money and war. The five million Jews in the US account for over a third of the world-wide Jewish Diaspora, yet amazingly they make up just two per cent of the American population. American Jews are generally cast as a group possessing power and influence immensely disproportionate to its size. The arguments are well known: Jews own all the banks, they run Hollywood and the media, Jews pull the strings in Congress, and influence Middle Eastern policy in a way that guarantees continued support for Israel over the Palestinians.

"Congress has passed resolutions that are more right-wing than the Likud Party in Israel," asserted a Muslim man whom I met at a mosque shortly after September 11th. As far as he was concerned, the so-called "Jewish lobby" was running Middle East policy and had been for years. If Congress started to show any sympathy towards the Palestinians, the powerful Jews would rein it back in, quicker than you could bake Matzah. The reason for this, he was convinced, was that Jews, or more correctly Zionists, were the biggest financial contributors to the American political system.

Jewish immigrants have done well in America. Like the Irish, they came out of crisis and pulled themselves up by their bootstraps. Any Jewish person I know is a lawyer, an entrepreneur or an opinion-former — all high achievers who, I suspect, just wouldn't know how to do it any other way. It's also true that in seeking support for Israel, they run one of the most effective lobbying organisations in the world. AIPAC (the American Israeli Political Action Committee) according to its own website has eighty-five thousand activists in the US. It claims that its work helps up to one hundred resolutions supporting Israel get passed in Congress every year. AIPAC even has a team of people dedicated to educating politicians on Capitol Hill and its annual conferences regularly attract speakers of the calibre of Bill or Hillary Clinton or Condoleezza Rice. The lobby's membership structure is like a presidential election committee, graded according to the size of a member's financial donation. The more money someone can give, the more insider access they are granted. A one thousand dollar membership entitles a donor to private briefings on issues affecting the relationship between the US and Israel. For six thousand dollars they will also get a trip to Israel to see the situation first-hand, while those who can stump up one hundred thousand dollars are entitled to all this, plus a private dinner date with the Vice President of the United States.

America in turn has poured billions of dollars into Israel to keep it secure and well off. Israel benefits from a kind of "best friend" status and is now also considered a vital ally on the front-lines of the war on terror. During his first term in office, President Bush resolutely refused to meet the then Palestinian leader Yasser Arafat, yet staged regular Rose Garden love-ins with Israel's Ariel Sharon, prompting accusations of bias. Bush saw Arafat as nothing more than a terrorist. Since the start of the fresh unrest that began in 2001, America has been slow to chastise Israel for violent army incursions into Palestinian territory, often serving as the lone voice against UN statements of condemnation.

But to even suggest that the Jewish lobby in the US has too much clout prompts accusations of anti-Semitism. This was made clear to me on a visit to the Israeli Embassy in Washington. To get in there was quite a job in itself. The multi-layered security system at the bullet-proofed building on Massachusetts Avenue made the White House look positively lax. "Jews have the right to organise and lobby just like the gun-owners or any other group," spokesman Mark Regev told me. To single out the Israeli lobby, he thought, smacked of anti-Semitism.

Despite vastly different takes on religion and on Jesus, America's Jews and Christians have forged strong relationships both on practical and religious matters. Evangelical Christians in particular believe that the Bible puts an onus on them to help Jews. If they are good to Israel, they believe that in turn they will receive blessings. In America, the best way to be good is to empty your pockets since your cash generally speaks louder than anything else. For years, evangelical churches have been raising money and passing it to groups like the Christian Jewish Fellowship to help return Jews to Israel. For three hundred and fifty dollars, the Fellowship will bring a Jew from the farthest corners of Russia back to Israel. Once arrived, other groups help with settlement. A Fellowship video being shown at Christian churches showed a destitute elderly Jewish couple somewhere in Eastern Europe sobbing as they begged to be allowed return to the land of their ancestors. Blackened pots and other debris were strewn around a hovel behind them. The woman was dressed in rags and the man wore a sweatshirt which read "Sky Sports" across the chest. No doubt they would have gone to Timbuktu to escape their misery, but somewhere back in America a congregation was being moved to tears and depositing money into a bucket. The video ended with the ecstatic couple bending down and kissing the ground as they arrived in Israel, perhaps to be settled on some disputed arid hillside beneath a security fence.

For many Americans George Bush is the President who has best represented Israel in recent times. Though Bill Clinton tried hard to strike a deal to end the Arab-Israeli conflict, he ultimately failed. Since September 11th, President Bush has redefined the problem as part of the war on terror. His simplification of one of the most complex problems of our times has allowed him to focus mainly on Israel's right to defend itself from suicide bombers. This unwavering support, however, is seen by many Muslims as evidence for their belief that the war on terror is a joint offensive by the US and Israel against Islam.

Despite his support for Israel, American Jews didn't support President Bush and generally vote Democrat. According to the American Jewish Committee, he received just twenty per cent of the Jewish vote in 2000 and slightly more in 2004. His vocal support for a Palestinian state has gone down well with some Jewish voters, who see this as a possible solution, though the more Orthodox and Zionist Jews disagree, but his handling of the war on terror has annoyed them. The committee has found that well over half of Jewish voters believe that the threat of terrorism has been increased as a result of his actions. George W. Bush would like nothing more than to go into the history books as the man who helped bring an end to the Palestinian conflict. His comments during our meeting in June 2004 indicated this, but also showed that he very much sees the conflict as just one part of the war on terror.

Even President Bush's strongest supporters are split on his handling of the Arab–Israeli conflict. Evangelical Christians believe that Israel must be protected to fulfil the key Bible prophecy: that when the Jews are all safely back in their homeland, Christ will come again and the Rapture will occur, lifting the saved to heaven and leaving the rest for the apocalypse. For them, the creation of the state of Israel in 1948 was the first step in the fulfilment of that prophecy. So while most evangelicals are happy to have a president who looks as if he understands all this, some believe that by supporting the abandonment of Jewish settlements or the creation of a Palestinian state, the President will hurt God's chosen nation and frustrate the biblical plan.

An evangelical Christian I had met at a religious event in New York was so furious with the President that she was carrying around a sign urging Americans to oppose any pullouts from settlements. Some Orthodox Jews objected to the forced removal of settlers from the Gaza Strip in August 2005 but the evacuation was supported by the majority of America's Jewish community, who hope it might be a step towards an eventual resolution.

"The Palestinians were given Jordan; they already have their Arab-Palestinian state," the woman I met in New York wailed. According to her, even the US Joint Chiefs of Staff had advised decades earlier that Israel could only be defensible if it retained Judea, Samaria, Gaza and the Golan. Given that Israel covers such a tiny part of the Middle East, she could not fathom how America, the EU, the UN and Russia were all demanding that parts of it be given up for Islam.

"Justice is always denied to the Jewish people," she shouted into my tape recorder.

OUR MOCK PASSOVER SEDER at the Aleph Bet School in Annapolis turned out to be a lively affair. Fifty hyped-up kids and their parents sat at long tables in the school gym where we had attempted to bake Matzah. Children were called to the stage to replay scenes from Exodus and performed a hilarious mime act in which they were attacked by a plague of insects as described in the scriptures. I sat at the back near two nine-year-old boys who bit the tops off all the plastic forks on the table and made strange noises to one another throughout the Seder. One boy was from a Reform Jewish family, the son of a Jewish mother and a Catholic father. "I just want him to know about his heritage," his mother explained. The others boy's inattention was put down to the fact that he was used to real Seders at home and was just bored silly. When the fried chicken came, however, everyone perked up, except that now none of us had any forks. We made do with our fingers. Instead of the four cups of wine that are traditionally drunk at a Seder, we drank grape juice. We ate parsley dipped in salt water to symbolise the tears of our ancestors. We leaned to one side while eating, to show that we are just as good as the Romans, who ate lying down. We sang songs and munched on factory-made Matzah.

Of all the faiths I had encountered as I journeyed through America, this was the one I had become most personally involved with. Being told that I was Jewish back at the bar in New

Hampshire was probably responsible for that. I can no longer claim to be ignorant of my heritage and no doubt Jhon Berenstein, my great-great-grandfather, would be chuffed that a descendant from Ireland was curious enough to find out a little about how he might have lived back in Latvia. I keep in contact with Rabbi Light and his wife and want to learn more; but, even with all that Catholic guilt over forgotten Mysteries of the Rosary and steaks enjoyed on Fridays, I will stay where I am, where breadcrumbs can roll underneath the fridge and stay there until Christmas if they want.

Chapter 12

God's Machine Gun

*I*F ROME HAS THE POPE and Tibet has the Dalai Lama, then America is surely the home of the televangelist. Surf through your television channels and before long you will find him there. Dressed in a double-breasted business suit, he is suave yet steely. With a shake of his fist, he will terrorise you and then calmly reassure you that everything is going to be alright. He wants your ear and your money and in exchange will relieve you of your heaviest burden and point you in the direction of the great redeemer. That's if you haven't yet changed the channel.

America's presidents and politicians, its sports stars and artists have all earned their place in world history but when it comes to religious leaders, few figures, apart from Martin Luther King Jr, have stood out — until now. After six decades of Bible-thumping, the Protestant evangelist Billy Graham is unquestionably America's premier preacher. More than any other individual, he has been responsible for the recent resurgence of Christianity across the United States and his public crusades have been the catalyst for the burgeoning "born again" movement. He has well earned his nickname: "God's Machine Gun".

No one else could get away with advertising a major religious rally as a "crusade". In the emotional days after September 11th, George W. Bush let the dreaded word tumble from his lips and suddenly America was in a war against Islam. But when Billy Graham spoke of a crusade, nobody batted an eyelid. He has been prosecuting his holy war for decades with one purpose in mind — saving souls. According to the Billy Graham Evangelistic Association, well over three million Americans have been "born again" at the preacher's public events.

I joined the throngs on the New York subway heading out of the city to Queens for Graham's last crusade there in June 2005. He was eighty-six years old and ailing and the word was this might be the end of the line for the revival road show. Half a century earlier, as a young hellfire-and-brimstone evangelist, he had filled New York's Madison Square Garden every night for two straight months. This time, he wanted to take over Central Park, but the city turned him down, directing the crusade instead to a park in Flushing Meadows. The Christians couldn't get into much trouble out there.

Waiting for the number seven train to Queens on a sweltering Sunday, it was easy to see why a soul-saving session in Central Park on that particular day could have been a disaster. On Fifth Avenue, the annual Gay Pride Parade was about to kick off, a multi-coloured carnival of quirkiness and queerness that would surely send Graham to an early grave and bring every satellite truck and reporter in the country rushing to New York for the live event of the year: "God versus the gays". America's culture war would spill onto the streets. Seeing the first of the latex-clad marchers arriving for the parade swinging their feather boas, I did think twice about getting on the train. Fifth Avenue would surely be more entertaining than where I was going; but then again, maybe not. It was a difficult choice between the queens in Manhattan and the Queens across the East River. But I decided to stick to my original plan. When the train glided to a halt in front of me, I boarded it.

GETTING IN TO THE CRUSADE in Flushing Meadows was a religious experience in itself. As hordes of spirited seekers moved from buses and trains towards the entrance, they were met by doomsday merchants advertising the end of the world. I grabbed a leaflet from one of them which outlined the sequence of events that supposedly will lead to World War III. The first shots will be fired with Egypt attacking Israel. This will be followed by Russia and China attacking Egypt and Africa. Nuclear weapons will be used and all the above will be destroyed. The apocalyptic prophecy, which the leaflet claimed was based on divine revelations by Our Lady in the 1970s, stated that these events would clear the way for the second coming of Christ.

After digesting this news, I was relieved to be next waylaid by a smiling, grandmotherly type wondering if I would be interested in joining her group. It would merely involve divesting myself of all worldly possessions, learning to play a musical instrument and moving to upstate New York to live in a commune with eighty others. "A lot of us used to be part of mainstream churches," she explained, "but we didn't want to do it on just Sundays and Wednesdays. We wanted to live the gospel, loving one another in a communal setting as Jesus wants us to." I knew a few tunes on the concert flute but was anxious to know what I would do for a living if I followed her.

"A lot of our work is in the construction business," she said, adding helpfully that they also run a number of local cafés. Tasks are divided among the members according to their individual talents, and women were needed to home-school the children. The smiling grandmother was called Zaviyth, a Hebrew name she had taken on joining the group. She was originally from New

Hampshire and with her husband had raised two children in a communal setting. Her six grandchildren were all being raised similarly. The lifestyle, she claimed, is a simple one with no drugs, alcohol or divorce allowed and no gays.

Chatting with her and others from the group, called the Litmus Test, it seemed to me that new brands of back-to-basics fundamentalism were springing up every week in America — not the violent extremism associated with terrorists but rather a rejection of the modern world.

"I suppose people are groping for something real in difficult times," reflected Greg Mitchell, a bearded man of about forty from Maine who had joined Zaviyth's community. He pointed to some of his fellow group members, a long-haired bunch with fiddles and banjos who could easily pass for a traditional Irish band. They had no specific view on the war in Iraq and without televisions didn't pay much attention to news or world events. "We don't vote or go to war," Zaviyth said. The Amish did not take part in war either but in some ways it all seemed too easy, dropping out of society and the responsibilities that come with it. "We're not like Amish; we live in communities and cities." Zaviyth stressed that their function in public life was to live by example and spread a light in the world. "The end won't come until the light is over the whole earth," she said, looking straight at me as if the "end" was something we should all be looking forward to. I still had the World War III leaflet in my hand and wondered if I should share the news with her, but it was time to move on or I would never get to see Billy Graham.

By EARLY AFTERNOON all seventy thousand seats in Flushing Meadows had been occupied. Somewhere the organisers had found seventy thousand folding chairs and set them up in rows with a view of either the main stage or a screen relaying the on-stage activity. The English-speaking section was already crammed, so I made my way to the much larger area set aside for immigrants. Here anyone having difficulty understanding the evangelist had the use of ear phones with translations in a variety of languages. I found a spot among the Koreans, a group I had previously encountered only at the dry cleaners — they seemed to be running every dry-cleaning shop in America. Koreans in general are very prim and proper, polite and business-like. Even those on moderate or low incomes dress immaculately. One woman arrived in a chic black dress, designer shoes and a hat, as if she were attending a wedding. But this was a crowded city park and by the time the event got started, the shoes were off and the dress was looking rather uncomfortable in the ninety degree heat. The man supervising the Korean section estimated that there were now three hundred thousand of them living in New York. Christianity, he confirmed, was gaining ground not just among Koreans in the US but back home in South Korea, thanks in part to Billy Graham, who had held crusades there going back as far as the end of the Korean War.

This was the first mass event I had seen where white Americans were totally outnumbered. Asians and Hispanics are establishing themselves in the Big Apple and many of them care deeply about their faith. Jesus may be domiciled in Red America right now, but that could change as immigrants breathe life back into abandoned inner-city churches. And not just Protestant evangelical churches. Catholic churches in the cities are also busy baptising new adult members, mainly from Asia. Contrary to the general view that New York is godless, in some areas of the city faith is just as vibrant as it is in the Bible Belt.

For years American televangelists have reached out beyond the United States to global audiences. Pat Robertson's Christian Broadcasting Network is based in Virginia but can be viewed in Latin America and Asia. A computer science student from the Dominican Republic told me that his family had been regular viewers of Robertson's syndicated programme, *The 700 Club*, back home. The daily television show, which presents Christian news and views, had actually motivated them to join the church. Unlike

Graham, Robertson had mixed preaching and politics and had made a run for the Republican presidential nomination in 1988, losing to George Bush Sr. As America grieved in the days after September 11th, Pat Robertson had rubbed salt in the wounds by claiming that the attacks were divine retribution for the sexual immorality in the United States. Many had believed him. Once again in August 2005 he alerted the world to his extreme views when he called for the assassination of Venezuelan President Hugo Chavez, another world leader irking America with his domestic policies and his support for Cuba — and inconveniently sitting on top of huge oil reserves.

This was day three of the New York crusade and some people had been there for the duration. Revivals take place over a number of days to give participants plenty of time to experience a "conversion". But, as with everything else, attention spans have shortened. In 1956, Graham gave New Yorkers eight weeks to hear the small voice inside. Here, the Holy Spirit would have to work his magic in seventy-two hours. On the second night of the event Bill and Hillary Clinton turned up for religion and some valuable publicity. "I love this man," the former President told the cheering crowd, as he reached out and took Graham's frail hand. The preacher had been careful not to hitch his wagon to either Democrats or Republicans. He had been invited to the White House by every president since Harry Truman, offering spiritual advice to those who would take it and just friendship to those who wouldn't. He was, however, close to George Bush Sr, holidaying at his home in Maine. George W. Bush also claims that Graham had helped him turn his life around for the better. The Clintons, who are not best known for their religious credentials, were trying to make up for lost time. If Hillary is going to run for president, she will need to be able to demonstrate an empathy with believers. Though the wall between church and state remains in place for now, it is difficult to see how a presidential candidate who does not openly speak of a belief in God can win in America any time soon.

"I don't think it is religion, it's a relationship with Jesus Christ that people are seeking." Catherine Nelson from Queens explained the current outpouring of religiosity as she saw it. "September 11th got people looking for a purpose and I think they found it in Jesus," she added. A heavy-set woman with a pleasant face, Catherine claimed to have been saved as a child when a female missionary visited her school. She had come to Flushing Meadows for a sort of refresher course but was not expecting another born-again experience. "I like sitting here listening to the different languages; it gives me an idea of what heaven will be like," she smiled as she looked around at the foreign faces. Like the majority of evangelical Christians, she was no longer a member of a mainstream church. Methodist, Presbyterian and Episcopal denominations, I had deduced from many conversations, were neither offering the kind of salvation that Americans craved nor demanding the kind of effort they were prepared to put in to achieve it. As part of her personal commitment, Catherine Nelson spent several hours a week on the streets of New York singing and searching for lost souls.

September 11th had clearly jolted Americans into pondering their own mortality, but the catalogue of death in Iraq did not seem to bother its evangelical Christians quite so much. "We need to fight for liberty and freedom. America was founded on freedom of religion and being able to worship God in the way we believe. Iraq was a dictatorship that prevented liberty. Anywhere you can fight for liberty I am for it," Catherine said.

"Even if that means killing innocents?" I asked.

"Freedom is never free; liberty comes with a price. If you are not willing to fight for it, then it is not worth having."

During the weekend of Billy Graham's last crusade in New York, opinion polls were showing that, for the first time, a majority of Americans felt that the invasion of Iraq had been a mistake. With no clear end in sight, they no longer considered it worth the cost in lives or money. Yet there were plenty like Catherine Nelson still supporting the President's view that freedom was worth every drop of blood spilt — albeit someone else's blood. She didn't have any children to make up the shortfall in army recruitment and none of the key political figures involved could point to even one family member serving in Iraq.

Lee Hung, a young evangelical from Vietnam, was more sceptical about Iraq. He was too young to remember America's last controversial war, but he wasn't hopeful that this would turn out any better. Lee had been in New York for fifteen years and had become a Christian, leaving Buddhism behind in Vietnam. "Because I have the freedom to choose," he answered, when I asked why he had switched. Despite his lack of faith in the war in Iraq, he did share President Bush's ideal of liberty.

All afternoon Christian rock bands and motivational speakers kept the crowd entertained as they waited for the main event. The humidity was stifling and people used books, newspapers and anything they could find to fan themselves. A New York firefighter came on stage and spoke about September 11th. He had rushed to ground zero after the planes had struck and was there when the first of the Twin Towers came crashing down, trapping him and his colleagues under a heap of debris. After they eventually freed themselves, the second tower fell. He lost twenty-four friends and three hundred of his workmates. Most of America has cast the details of that day to the back of its collective mind. You rarely hear people in Kansas or Utah or Georgia casually mention September 11th or the Towers. It's almost as if they still can't believe it had happened that way. But in New York you can sometimes feel the raw emotion as if it had happened last week.

The firefighter was followed on-stage by a pastor who reminded the faithful that saving souls in New York cost money — seven million dollars to be exact. "God loves a cheerful giver," he roared, exhorting them to dig deep for the Lord. When the big white crusade buckets came around, they were quickly filled with cash, cheques and pledge cards.

Then, as if direct from heaven, Billy Graham appeared.

HIS HAIR IS SNOW WHITE and a little too long. The thin face looks old and tired but the man's clear blue eyes seem to light him up from the inside. At eighty-six years of age, he is no longer able to stand or wave his hands or thump his fists. His shout is gone too. "If I died right now, I would go straight to heaven and see Jesus," he told the crowd, from his seated position. The people yelled like rock fans hearing the opening bars of a song they had been waiting for.

"We are approaching a climactic moment in history. There is going to come an end to the world." Graham looked out at his flock. This "end", he explained, would be like the great flood back in Noah's day, which had come at a time when corruption and violence were widespread. Somewhat prophetically, from an evangelical worldview, Graham was speaking nine weeks before Hurricane Katrina would bring a flood of almost biblical proportions to New Orleans, but that city's Superdome, to which the masses were directed, would prove to be a poor substitute for Noah's ark, with reported gunfire and looting.

"What would it have been like if there was twenty-four-hour news back in Noah's time?" Graham posed the question rhetorically, guessing that Noah would have been laughed out of it for making such grim predictions and that the weather channel would have reassured people that no storm could wreak that much havoc. Graham then recited stories from that Sunday's news — three young boys found suffocated in the trunk of a car, a young girl murdered. The only good news he could see was the coming of Christ.

"I believe he is coming."

Another huge cheer went up around the park.

"Are you ready?"

"YES!" The audience, which now numbered almost ninety thousand, shouted back. "YES!" The normally reserved Koreans were on their feet and roaring back at him.

"There will come a day when you will hear a gigantic noise from heaven," he went on, his voice gaining strength. "At that moment the dead will rise from their graves all across New York. But we will be divided. Some will be eternally lost, some eternally saved."

There it was — the core of Graham's message for six decades and the nub of what the evangelical movement believes. The day of reckoning is not a joke. Some people will be left behind. There is no doubt that tens of thousands of people in that stadium feared that they would be among them. That is probably why they were there. But Graham had a way to beat it.

"We are saved through Jesus if we put our faith in him," he continued, strongly advising the crowd that today should be the day to take up this offer. Like a true salesman, he gave them the hard sell, hypothesising that if anyone in Flushing Meadows was to be killed by a bus on their way home that night, they would have missed their shot at salvation.

"I want you to get out of your seat and come to this platform and say, 'Tonight I want Jesus'."

This is what evangelists describe as the "altar call", the moment at which those who have decided to start anew are expected to walk up to the stage in front of everyone and make their commitment. With a choir providing suitable background music, people gingerly began to move out of their seats. It wasn't a mass movement, but a steady stream.

"You have not come to me," the evangelist emoted, his voice now adopting a dream-like quality. "You have come to Jesus and he receives you." Suddenly the park went very quiet. There were no emotional histrionics, no crying or speaking in tongues, just several hundred people, maybe a thousand, standing silently at Graham's altar. I looked around for any sign of Bill or Hillary Clinton, but they hadn't made it back for this.

"Oh God, I am a sinner and I am sorry for my sins. I am willing to turn away from those sins. . . ." Graham asked those before him to repeat his words. It was practically the same prayer Catholics recite after confession and it struck me that the business of being saved, which had intrigued and even intimidated me since arriving in America, was little different from what I had done countless times in dark damp confessionals, without the music or the dreamy white-haired preacher. As a child I had been eager to march in there every Saturday afternoon to report to the priest that "I cursed". As I grew up, this had been replaced by more infrequent and more vague pronouncements such as, "It's not what I did, Father; it's what I didn't do."

Despite his fiery reputation, Billy Graham's style of repentance is a lot less stressful. No one had to recite any sins or weaknesses here or sit alone in a dark box wondering who or what was behind the grille.

After the altar call, trained helpers took over the salvation process, handing out copies of the gospels and taking names and phone numbers of the newly reborn. The drill was to get them to a church as quickly as possible before the desire to remain saved wore off. Everyone who had being saved was assured that they would be phoned within forty-eight hours by someone who could direct them to a pastor. Most of Graham's helpers were talking to teenaged children and recent immigrants who probably didn't belong to any church yet. To them, the day was like a baptism, except they were choosing it freely. Evangelicals generally don't baptise babies, which is why most of their children get "saved" in their early teens. But had I not also received confirmation, the gift of the Holy Spirit, at that age? Wasn't it the same thing? I too had been saved, and by a bishop, hadn't I?

It's what comes after this that separates America's evangelicals from the majority of Christians such as Catholics or mainstream Protestants. From the time a person commits to an evangelical church in America, they are schooled in the Bible. Not just a parable here and there; they read it systematically, discussing it and learning it until they can repeat entire verses. What evangelicals prove is that regular reading of the Bible shapes their lifestyle and their views and makes them morally conservative.

Not everyone at Graham's last crusade was an evangelical. I spoke to Roman Catholics and members of the Russian Orthodox faith, mostly drawn by their admiration for the man. "He speaks to the entire world, not just Christians, and his message is the same for everybody," observed an elderly woman from the Midwest who together with her husband had sat through three full days. Graham believes that God does not discriminate between faiths. He refused to take the rap for his son Franklin Graham, also an evangelist, who had publicly described Islam as "a wicked and evil" religion. The elder Graham did make amends for taped comments made decades previously in conversation with Richard Nixon, in which they had accused Jewish media owners of spreading a culture of pornography and smut.

Rather than shunning the media, as so many religious leaders do, Graham embraced television and radio, paving the way for generations of evangelists. His broad appeal and his willingness to use mass communications have in a sense made him America's Pope — a Baptist Pope. While Graham and Pope John Paul II disagreed on many theological issues, both men have been recognised as unique individuals who stayed on message as long as their health would allow. Both travelled extensively and both suffered in public. John Paul II's struggle to keep going in the face of such humiliating disabilities moved America — not just its sixty million Catholics. And Graham's frailty contrasts so sharply with his early days that he too will be remembered for his struggle.

LEAVING THE PARK I TOOK ONE WRONG TURN and got siphoned off into the path of a Seventh-Day Adventist who wanted to preach some more.

"What are you going to tell me that I didn't hear from Mr Graham?" I asked, anxious to break free and get home. "America is becoming a moral majority and that's dangerous," he answered. "You will soon see a national Sunday law," he added, putting forward a theory that government would sanction Sunday as the official Sabbath and a day of rest. The problem was not that he wanted to shop on Sundays — his complaint was that the Sabbath was on Saturday, not Sunday. "Right," I took his leaflet, promised to study it, and made my escape into the crush for the train back to Manhattan.

Back in the city, America's cherished freedom had allowed thousands of gays, lesbians and transsexuals to celebrate their uniqueness. Fifth Avenue had been a riot of colour, with flamboyant characters dressed in over-the-top costumes, attracting large crowds of bemused spectators. One stray fairy ended up at the Billy Graham event dressed all in white, presumably to make the point that gays want to marry. The fairy carried a magic wand which will probably be needed if this wish is ever to come true.

Thanks to the quick thinking of the city, which kept these moral and ideological opposites apart, there was no unpleasantness. It's not that America's homosexuals hate its evangelicals, or even the other way around. The problem is more that they are scared of one another. Each group fears that the other is out to destroy its freedoms. For homosexuals, that is the freedom to live as they choose with the same rights as everyone else. For the conservative Christians it means the freedom not to have to deal with homosexuals openly parading the gay lifestyle in front of them or their children.

"I don't brag to them about my sex life," Kay O'Connor, an elderly teacher back in Kansas, had replied when I asked her why she felt so threatened. "I don't want to hear about theirs."

Gay marriage, abortion and stem cell research will remain at the centre of the moral war being fought in America. But no one will win.

Freedom is not absolute. It involves compromises on both sides. And it's hard to believe that salvation is guaranteed to anyone who does not show some compassion to others. Travelling through this country, I had to wonder sometimes if "Love thy neighbour", the key commandment, has gone out of fashion.

God's Machine Gun has gone silent on all this. Maybe old Billy Graham is waiting to discuss it in person with the man above.

Chapter 13

The End of the World

THEY SAY NOTHING CAN PREPARE YOU for the Grand Canyon. So I didn't prepare. Instead I hopped on an evening flight from Baltimore to Las Vegas, clambered into a rented Chevy, hightailed it out of Nevada at midnight, slept at a roadside hotel in Arizona, crossed the Hoover Dam and drove clear through the desert right to the Canyon's edge.

So there I was. And for the life of me, I didn't know what to think. Ten miles wide, two hundred and seventy-seven miles long, and all I could muster up was a faint "Gee". At first.

The sun was at its highest, the time of day when it's difficult to make out the shape and contour of something so incredibly vast. For several minutes I just stood trying to focus my eyes on the gaping crater until I began to feel strangely self-conscious. It seemed as though the Canyon was looking back at me. The longer I stared, the more I felt as if I was standing alone on the stage of the world's biggest auditorium. There was not just one pair of eyes trained on me; there were hundreds, thousands even. I was face to face with ancient kings resting on massive stone armchairs, peach-coloured angels, dark devils, gods and goddesses, all still, all silent and all staring.

Call it paranoia, but I swear the Grand Canyon knows you are looking at it. Something bothered me though. I couldn't figure out how I was going to get acquainted with this monster. How could I touch it and smell it and search its nooks and crannies? There were too many of them and they were so unreachable. As a journalist, I had been used to getting the insider's look, used to getting as close to my subject as possible, but I knew that in this place I was as much an outsider as the next person, and it would take more than a brief visit to change that.

So, six thousand years old or four and a half billion? That's the first question I would have asked if I thought those stone gods could answer. For months I had been asking people all over America about the origin of the planet and had achieved nothing near a consensus. I had encountered the creationists — mainly but not exclusively conservative Christians — who believe the world was made by God in six days a few thousand years back, just like it says in the Book of Genesis. Then there is science, which says that a place like the Grand Canyon was fashioned by layers of rock settling one upon the other for billions of years. Even the upper levels of the Canyon, alternating layers of sandstone, shale and limestone, are thought to have been deposited up to six hundred million years ago. Then the Colorado River had to slice through the layers of rock for five million more years to create the deep canyon fissure. At points along the ridge, where you can catch a glimpse of the river, it appears as narrow as a string of dental floss, but at certain points it is three hundred feet wide.

"Oh don't get me started on that." That's what Kelly Coleman, the Christian missionary I had met in Midland, Texas, had said when I asked for his thoughts on creation versus evolution. We were at the Petroleum Museum, looking at displays on how oil had come to be in the ground beneath Texas. From a scientific point of view, it appeared to have been a process that took quite some time but this didn't fit in with the Christian view of things. "Maybe a bit of both," he concluded.

The debate over creation has spilled over into America's schools and into public life. Conservative states in the centre of the country, such as Kansas and Arkansas, want school textbooks to state that evolution is just a theory on how the world came to be. Two-thirds of Americans now believe that creationism should be taught in school, though not all of them agree that it deserves equal weight with Darwin's theory.

"I think it's intelligent design," Mormon writer Dan Witherspoon had told me in Salt Lake City. There was always some sort of matter out there, he felt, but it was God who had coaxed it into becoming intelligent life. The intelligent design movement holds, for example, that the human eye is far too complex a system to have happened by accident or evolution.

There is a group to support every possible theory. There are the modern geo-centrists, who believe that God created a spherical earth and put it at the centre of the universe; the flat-earth creationists; and the day-age creationists who subscribe to the theory that it was all done and dusted in six days — but that each day lasted for millions of years.

As I made my way along the southern rim of the Canyon, the afternoon sun gave way to the watery evening light that everyone who makes the journey here raves about. Already the rocks were shedding their noonday haze and taking on a more reddish hue. At a lookout point a crowd of people were focusing their binoculars and cameras on something on the rocks below. A secondary crowd was quickly gathering to see what the first crowd was looking at.

"It's a Californian condor," announced a man who was snapping away with an impressive telephoto lens.

"Very rare," added a woman, also shooting off rolls of film. Someone lent me a set of binoculars and, after much pointing of fingers, I could make out a large black bird with a flesh-coloured neck perched on a ledge about an eighth of a mile down. The owner of the binoculars, a biology teacher from Illinois, was beside himself with excitement. Up to a few years ago, he said, there had been just twenty-two of these condors left but a number of them had been taken into captivity, introduced to each other, and now there were over two hundred. There were gasps from the crowd as a second condor landed beside the first, alighting like a jet plane with its wheels down. Each bird was numbered and we were looking at numbers nineteen and twenty-two.

"Evolution or creation?" I asked the biology teacher.

"I think you know what I think," he said, before adding that he had become a Christian late in life. I had to assume he still held to the scientific theory, but he went on to explain that most of the young kids he was trying to teach science to now believed that God had created the world in six days and rested on the seventh.

It was almost sunset, and a large group of people had staked out spots on a flat overlook known as Yavapai Point. Sitting among them was like being inside the tower of Babel, as languages from every corner of the world melded into a low stream of chatter. There were Germans, French, Indians, Spaniards, Mexicans, Russians and a large contingent of Chinese and Japanese. The talking subsided and cameras were positioned for the moment when the sun would spread like a pinky orange glaze right across the rim. There was a burst of shutters clicking and lenses zooming as the final rays of light hit the depths, bathing the stone kings in phosphorescent pyjamas, for just a few seconds before everything went dark.

It was at this point that I heard the singing. In a corner, three young people were belting out a hymn *a cappella*. "God's wounds have paid my ransom" they sang. After all my travels, these words were now familiar to me. They were singing about being saved. Just like everywhere else I had been, the evangelicals were making themselves heard while everybody else kept their thoughts to themselves. "When it's this beautiful, you just have to sing and praise God," one of the girls smiled.

THE NEXT DAY, MY SKIN COVERED in factor 50 sun block and armed with several bottles of water, I did tackle part of the Canyon, hiking down the first part of the Bright Angel trail. As a reference, I kept my eye fixed on a boat-shaped stone edifice in the middle of the Canyon known as "the battleship". After two and a half hours, I was level with my target and satisfied that I had gone some way into the belly of this beast, though I was no more than a third of the way down. I resolved to go the whole way next time and book a bed at Phantom Ranch, the hostel by the Colorado River where the serious hikers stay. An elderly couple who overtook me on the climb back up had been hiking for a week crossing from south rim to the north and back again. The smile on their faces indicated that they would be dining out on their achievement for a long time.

I had merely dipped my toe into the Grand Canyon, yet I found it a difficult place to leave. There is something in those rocky depths that draws you in.

Driving away from it, I stopped at every single overlook to drink in just one more view. At one of these, I instantly did a double take. Yards in front of me, two black condors were just hanging about on a rocky promontory. Clearly visible on their wings were the numbers nineteen and twenty-two, the same two birds the crowds had watched and photographed with such awe the night before. I must have been getting light-headed in the ninety degree heat because I imagined that they had followed me and, like Navajo spirits, were trying to communicate something. Keep travelling. Or maybe go home. Who knows.

At Desert View, the final overlook at the western end of the Canyon, I stopped at the visitors' centre located in a tall stone tower. Walking from the Chevy towards the visitors' centre, I noticed a slight commotion. An overweight man in Bermuda shorts was yelling something up at the tower, and a few more people stood behind him as if backing him up. But everyone else seemed to be standing around laughing. I would never have believed it if I had not seen it with my own eyes, but there was one of the condors, number twenty-two, trying to get in the window of the visitors' centre. The black bird was much too large for the narrow window ledge and had spread its huge wings against the glass to achieve a precarious balance. Inside, the incredulous faces of the visitors were pressed up to the pane. So much for my Indian spirits theory; this rarest of rare birds had been so tamed by captivity that it just wanted someone to take it home.

ROUTE 89 SOUTH FROM THE CANYON takes you through the Navajo nation. Much of Arizona is American Indian territory and what strikes the passer-by is the crushing poverty. Indian homes are generally scattered in the most inhospitable and nondescript desert places and there never seems to be much in the way of commerce going on around them. I had previously visited a Paiute reservation in Nevada where slot machines and fireworks had established themselves as the main source of livelihood. Land and nature, once the source of everything to the American Indian, was now more often than not the source of bitter legal battles. In a dusty parking lot a few miles from the end of the Grand Canyon, I came across a group of elderly women with brown wrinkled faces, patiently waiting for a chance to exchange some home-made turquoise jewellery for a few dollars. For a half an hour I was their only customer.

I followed the road past the snow-capped San Francisco mountain peaks to Flagstaff and from there drove on through the Coconino forest to Sedona, which was for me one of the most remarkable spots in the entire United States. Entering Sedona, the rocks suddenly turn the colour of terracotta and angle up against the sky in the oddest of shapes. The town itself is surrounded on all sides by the red rock formations and has a quaint western feel. It is also a magnet for New Age thinkers and spiritual seekers.

I checked into a Best Western Hotel and grabbed a handful of pamphlets from the front desk. There was enough hokey stuff here to keep me busy for months. At the Center for the New Age, I could avail of the services of clairvoyants and psychics, have my aura photographed or receive messages from angels. If none of these did anything for me, I could try past-life regression, shamanic counselling or soul retrieval. There were tours to the mountains, where I could experience a vortex, join a drumming circle or attend a full moon ritual.

The next day being Sunday, I started off as traditionally as I could. I attended a Roman Catholic Mass, said by a priest wearing cowboy boots and one of those lip microphones attached to a headset that pop stars use during dance routines. The congregants hugged the priest as they filed out afterwards. No reserved "good morning, Father" or "nice sermon" comments here. This was a decidedly touchy-feely affair.

After Mass I followed the directions on one of the pamphlets to the Center for Creative Life. The building, constructed of adobe and glass, was located in an exquisite setting at the base of the mountains on the outskirts of Sedona. Inside, a group of about a dozen people were listening to a man called Damon Catizone talk about the alignment of the planets. He looked like a guru of some sort, the type that can tell you in three easy steps how to shed your miserable past and your debts. His white hair and beard contrasted sharply with his dark eyes and black clothing. He too wore a microphone as he strode over and back across the stage. Death, Catizone told his audience, is just an illusion. None of us, he claimed, would ever die, we would simply progress to the next plane.

"Ooooommm . . ." he had everyone humming as he finished up with some meditation before sweeping out the door without any hugs or handshakes. I found him in a little bookshop at the front of the building and tried my question about the origin of the world on him. "It was created and evolved and continues to evolve," he answered, without even pausing to think. Call it God, or space, or life, he felt there was one source of existence. We were all "shot out" from this source as divine sparks and then entered into matter. We were, he was sure, now passing through the human kingdom — the lower kingdom — from where we would progress out of matter again and up to the higher kingdom. This was yet another theory which seemed to combine what the Christians and the scientists thought.

"Does Jesus come into it?" I asked.

"He had a role to play — to bring love to humanity."

Damon was a child of the 1960s, though it was hard to tell if he had "inhaled" or not. He had started out in the construction business in California, dabbling in a bit of sculpture on the side. A lapsed Roman Catholic, he had met Torkom, an Albanian living in America, whom he referred to as a great teacher of ageless wisdom. Catizone and Torkom had meandered through life together until the teacher died. Now it was the Californian's turn to help spread the wisdom. "Young people want truth, not just Bible parables," he believed, stressing that New Age theories are gaining ground. Though his audience in the auditorium had been small and middle-aged, he felt that more Americans feel that traditional churches have served their purpose and that their time has passed.

TRAVELLING THOUGH RURAL AMERICA, I had been struck by the number of people who felt the world was coming to an end. For a start, tens of millions of evangelical Americans were counting on the Rapture, the event they say is prophesised in the Bible. They are fully expecting that in the not-too-distant future Jesus will return and take his chosen ones with him, leaving the rest to perish.

"I think we are in the very last days," Kelly Coleman had warned me back in his office in Midland, Texas. Kelly, who had attended Bible study with President Bush, subscribed to the apocalyptic theory. "The Book of Revelations talks about how wars will increase, earthquakes will increase and when you see these things happen you'll know it's the time, it's the season."

"So if it's all about to end, what's your function?" I had asked him.

"Our function is to get as many people saved from hell as we can. There's people going to hell. . . ."

In Utah, the Mormons had talked of Christ returning soon for a thousand-year reign of peace on earth; and the Jews subscribe to an era of peace and prosperity coinciding with the coming of a yet-to-be-revealed Messiah. For some of these groups modern-day events such as the legalisation of abortion in 1973 or the establishment of the state of Israel in 1948 were all clear signs of the end of days. I had found countless others who lived with a similar philosophy. Menno, the Amish horse-and-buggy driver back in Intercourse, Pennsylvania, had told me he was surprised that God has not come yet: "We thought he would have come by now." Across the US border in Mexico, I had encountered the indigenous people waiting for something to happen in December 2012 when, according to the Mayan timetable, the current phase of creation ends. And the United Effort Plan, a group of polygamist Mormons in the south-western US, had felt cheated and disappointed that the world didn't end on 6 April 2005. They had built a new temple in the Texas desert especially for the event.

Everyone with strict religious beliefs seemed to be looking forward to the end, not dreading it. It was as if they had become fed up with their own culture and were hoping for something better to come. In the meantime they all felt a need to draw back, to slow down, and to focus on what they felt was really important. Most I met were doing so through their religion or their lifestyle.

Damon Catizone, the ageless wisdom teacher, doesn't believe the world will be ending any time soon. All the religious theories surrounding this, he claimed, are mistaken. What is really happening is that the world is simply moving out of the Piscean age and into the Aquarian age. The dawning of the age of Aquarius is already upon us, having begun about two hundred years ago and is set to last for a further two thousand three hundred years. The conflicts within America and around the world, he believes, are simply a sign of the old fanatical traditional viewpoints clashing with the new.

IGNORING CATIZONE'S ADVICE to avoid psychics and others operating on the astral plane, I drove back into Sedona to see what angel therapy was about. A class was due to start at one o'clock at a pastel pink and green building on the way into town. When I got there, however, the class had been cancelled because the air conditioning was broken, but Jocelyn, who was due to lead the session, was still available for consultations if I wished to find out more. As I waited, I scanned the shelves of books on the power of crystals, I Ching, Chakra balancing and other forms of spiritual and physical renewal. Despite the high proportion of Americans who call themselves believers, over eighty per cent, non-religious spirituality, often based on various versions of Eastern mysticism, is also on the rise. This has more to do with physical and mental wellbeing than attending church; more about stress reduction than doctrine. But like religion, it is a growing business. This spiritual supermarket opened its first branches in California and New York but has now spread right throughout the US and across the world. There are few spots remaining on the map where you can't commune with the spirits or journey inside yourself.

Jocelyn looked like a 1960s' hippy. She had long fair hair parted in the middle and wore a colourful smock dress. She exuded a motherly charm and spoke with confidence. I followed her up a flight of stairs to a small back room. She apologised for the lack of air conditioning but had rigged up a whirring electric fan in the corner, which was blowing everything about. She directed me to a chair opposite her at a small table and poured me a glass of water from a big flask — purifying water which she recommended that I drink. A crystal ball sat on the table alongside a small microphone attached to an intercom. (I had yet to meet somebody in Sedona who did not use a microphone!)

Immediately we were sidetracked away from the angels when she announced that she is in fact a fully fledged Wiccan priestess. Wicca, I knew from reading surveys on religion in America, is among the fastest-growing groups of all. Although its numbers are still under two hundred thousand, it appears to be poised to explode. Jocelyn's business is witchcraft and magic. The daughter of Mormon parents back in California, she had rebelled against that religion, found her own and moved to Arizona. Wicca is a polytheistic religion which worships the Goddess as well as the God and celebrates the cycles of nature. Wiccans have a simple view of the world. They believe that everyone should act according to their conscience. People should generally try to avoid hurting others and if they do harm to their neighbour, they will pay for it threefold. "And ye harm none, do as ye will" is their motto. It didn't seem all that outlandish.

"Do you have a broomstick?" I asked, stumped by my own lack of knowledge on the subject.

"Sure," she laughed, explaining that when her daughter was young, Hallowe'en at their house involved a little more than just trick or treating. "We would sit around the fire and contact our dead uncle; that impressed the other kids at school," she said. Her daughter, however, had not followed her into the witchcraft business. She had become a Buddhist instead. So Jocelyn's family had gone from Mormon to Wicca to Buddhism — the ultimate spiritual supermarket shoppers.

As a priestess, she has strong views about the way America is being led politically and spiritually. All the religious "nonsense" in the White House, she felt, was a cover expertly used by a group of people to serve their own self-interests. Anybody who still believes that the war on terror is not about oil, she felt, doesn't even deserve to have a vote.

"Look," she said, placing a straw into her flask of water. "For so long we have been the only ones sucking out of the straw. There's just a little bit left and suddenly the whole football team is crowding around looking for a drink."

China and India, she added, are the thirstiest members of the football team and will only get thirstier.

"It will have to come to a head in the next fifty years," she said, predicting more conflict over energy sources. "I give it five years," she added, without even glancing in the direction of the crystal ball. A message over the intercom indicated that she had a new customer coming up. I thanked her for her time and got up to leave. "I would like you to come to my house for dinner tonight, so we can talk further," she invited, catching me off guard. I muttered something to the effect that I would see how my day went, and get back to her later.

In the afternoon I headed out of town past the Chapel of the Holy Cross, one of the world's most spectacularly situated Roman Catholic churches. Shaped like a simple cross on the exterior, the chapel is built into the side of the mountain. A sculptress called Marguerite Brunswig had it designed and built in the 1960s in memory of her parents. Beyond the chapel the road winds around to Cathedral Rock and Bell Rock, both red rock mountains that have inspired mystics and sceptics alike. Beneath the bell-shaped one I sat down.

"Can't you feel it?"

The voice made me jump. I turned to see a women striding past me, heading towards the base of the rock.

"Feel what?" I asked.

"The vortex."

"A vortex? Where?"

"You are in it."

This vortex, supposedly, is an energy that develops around these rocks, affecting people in strange ways. I stood up on a rock and turned a full three hundred and sixty degrees. I was completely surrounded by haunting shapes which in the silence could lead you to feel as if you were being swept up by a supernatural something. People have reported being lifted off their feet, moved to tears or sent running by some invisible force in these rocks. Having being spared any of this, I was tempted to assume that a vortex is just another product on the spiritual supermarket shelf and whether or not you buy it depends on how badly you need it.

So much of what I had now seen convinced me that people just achieve their balance in different ways. Some believe they have a lock on the truth and have a duty to tell everybody else about it. Others just enjoy their karma quietly and hope for the best. But the whole of America seems to be searching for *some* kind of salvation as a solution to their problems. So many of the adults who claimed conversion experiences had stories to tell of how bad things had been — up until the time they found religion. Prisoners on death row get "saved" every day of the week. Alcoholics put down their bottles and take up Bibles. People driven close to suicide one day find a way to stick around and help others the next.

Likewise the attacks of September 11th, the Asian tsunami and increasingly devastating hurricanes have got a lot of Americans believing that the world could end soon and that it is time to prepare for the next life. A large majority of Americans believe in an afterlife and in heaven, a belief not nearly as strong in Europe. Having a purpose like this can be a powerful motivator. Ask Rick Warren, an evangelical pastor who wrote a book called *The Purpose Driven Life*. His forty-day programme, which he promises will reveal God's individual plan for every person who reads it, has become one of the biggest-selling books in publishing history. He claims that life is not about the individual but about how God wants to use each person to achieve something good. This message has caught on with tens of millions of Americans who have been turning sharply away from the "me first" mentality of the 1980s and 1990s. Other authors have made their name appealing to America's sense of apocalyptic fear. The *Left Behind* fiction series, based on the biblical account of the Rapture, has been flying off the shelves.

None of this is going to go away. As ordinary people become more apprehensive about how the world is turning out, they will depend even more on formulas, fads and faith to get them through. Some Americans are worried about terrorists taking their freedom; others about China taking their jobs. Many fear that the United States is in danger of losing its once glorious position as the land of opportunity and dreams. As people refine their beliefs to suit their own worldview, new churches are springing up. If they don't like what's already available, they can always start a new one. How about the Solid Rock Church, Church of the Golden Age, The Master Bible Church, Starlight Community Church, Unitarian Universalist Fellowship, Church of Christ Scientist, Rock of Ages Lutheran Church, First Assembly of God, United Methodist Church, Church of the Nazarene? All these were churches in Sedona. For a town with a population of ten thousand, there are thirty different varieties of worship. In other states, I had come across a biker's church on the side of the road and a trucker's chapel at a gas station. Anyone who couldn't find a venue for their church was setting one up in their own home — like Pope Michael of Kansas, who never attended any service outside his own attic. If I ever feel the need to have my own church, I could call it "The Church of the Wandering Scribes". Nice ring to it.

I decided not to join Jocelyn the Wiccan priestess for dinner at her home that evening in Sedona. I hope she wasn't insulted. It wasn't that I was afraid of what a woman who claims to be a witch might put on the table for dinner, or that we would spend the evening talking to her deceased uncle. I had come away from every believer and atheist I had met along the way enhanced in my knowledge. I just felt it was nearly time to end this journey. I could keep going for years and still only scratch the surface of how Americans see faith and religion and their place in this world and the next. It was time to go back east.

Chapter 14

For God and Country

$\mathcal{B}$ack in Annapolis, I have been waking to the sound of bells tolling on the quarter hour at the US Naval Academy church. My temporary digs are located just across the wall from the Academy and I can hear the shouts and grunts of the midshipmen going through their morning drill. A sprawling complex, looking out onto the bay, the Academy takes up a quarter of the town and is home to four thousand naval and marine officers in training. Unlike the casual charm of other college campuses, it is stern and dignified. Its gardens are methodically manicured, its brass knobs are shining and its inhabitants are polite, uniformed and always striving, always pushing themselves to the limit.

In the summer a brand new batch arrived, fresh-faced and eager. They will spend four years behind the wall, before going off to join the war on terror. Anyone coming to the Academy is making a long-term commitment. After graduation, they will serve Uncle Sam for a minimum of five years, though most will stay longer. With the way things are in Iraq, one wouldn't blame them if they stopped coming but, war or no war, twelve hundred idealistic youngsters from the fifty states have just checked in to begin their military career. After all, the government pays their expenses and who in their right mind would turn down the chance for three hundred thousand dollars' worth of free education? That's the cost of making an officer and a gentleman (or lady) out of an awkward teenager.

"Move it, move it, move it!"

"Yes, sir!"

"Now!"

"Aye Aye!"

That's how it went for the first day as the skinny, the short and the tall were shown around their new quarters. Each was given the bare essentials: bed sheets, a giant laundry bag, a selection of uniforms and a set of reef notes — a small book of military rules and slogans, to be committed to memory, without delay. The navy barber shaved their heads and the ones who couldn't see too well were issued with thick brown-rimmed glasses, infinitely uglier than anything the health service could ever pawn off on old-age pensioners. If that wasn't bad enough, they were now to be known as "plebes" — the lowest form of life in the naval hierarchy.

"We learned some stuff by screwing up and having people yell at us. That's pretty much it for today," Jonathan LeQuay from California summed up his introduction to the United States Navy.

"No excuse, sir!"

"I'll find out, sir!"

"Yes, sir!"

"No, sir!"

For the next eight weeks this would be the extent of his utterances to anyone ranked above him, which meant almost everyone. New recruits are trained and disciplined by those in the upper classes, known as the "firsties". No doubt they would encounter the odd "flamer" — the colloquial term for an upperclassman abusing his authority. Plebe LeQuay was unperturbed by the sudden switch from his breezy west coast life. He wanted to be there and he knew where he was headed. He would join the Marines, "the few, the proud", but he hadn't given much thought to the possibility of ending up fighting insurgents in Iraq.

"I think by the time we are out of here, in 2009, Iraq will be over," he said hopefully.

I couldn't find anyone else to agree with Plebe LeQuay. The consensus among parents and friends who were there to see the new midshipmen take their oath was that America could be bogged down in Iraq for a decade. And even if things do settle down there, trouble would surely pop up somewhere else. The night before, President Bush had addressed the nation in an attempt to shore up flagging support for the war. He needed more time and urged everyone to be patient. There would be little point in running now, he reasoned, leaving the terrorists to claim their bloody victory. Thirty months into the war and an average of thirty people a day were dying. But this focus on death, the President felt, was obscuring the real progress being made. If he thought things were going according to plan, some others felt it was high time to change the plan.

"I'm relieved I didn't have to hear any of his jargon here today," a retired officer commented as he prepared to watch the new recruits raise their right hands to solemnly take their oath to protect and defend America. He was from the class of 1965 and had served for seven years before being injured in Vietnam. "I just scraped through here too," he added, looking around the yard where he had once trained. He didn't envy the new generation starting out. "I'm so appalled by this administration," he said, before excusing himself.

A handsome new recruit and his father — also a Navy man — were happy to talk, until I asked them what they had thought of the President's speech. The boy winced and a kind of shadow came over the father's face as they tried to decide if they should answer. I had been interviewing Americans long enough to know that within the four walls of a military establishment, anyone who didn't jump to the defence of the Commander-in-Chief was trying to tell you something. The son, barely nineteen, looked nervously at his old man, willing him to keep his mouth shut.

"I take it that's a no comment?" I asked finally.

"Yes, no comment." Father and son jumped at the chance to avoid any further conversation on the matter.

"And we know what that means," I added, smiling, as I made to leave. Big mistake.

"No, that's an assumption, it's a no comment," the son said, showing his frustration that he even had to think about this today, never mind talk to a European journalist. "We just don't want to comment. That's all," he said.

HEATHER, A DIMINUTIVE YOUNG WOMAN from North Carolina, one of two hundred women in the new class, had to convince her family to let her come. "We've been apprehensive about this from the beginning. We wanted her to make another choice, but this was her decision," her mother said, looking deflated as the family sat in a little circle on the lawn saying their goodbyes. Heather had got stuck with the national health glasses and was drowning in her white midshipman's tunic. She was barely five feet tall and her sleeves were about four inches too long. Her sister, sitting next to her, was off to law school, a very sensible choice according to her mother. But she would never get to command an aircraft carrier. Heather just might.

A few days earlier I had met a Navy man who had been stationed on board a carrier the night the Iraq war started in March 2003. He said it had fallen to a twenty-three-year-old woman to direct the hulking ship out of port in San Diego and point it in the direction of the Gulf. "She was the oldest person up on the main deck that night," he said. As a chaplain ministering to these young Americans, he knew the excitement but he also knew the fear of serving in times of war. "They would be lined up waiting for confession, they thought they were going to die," he said of the sailors on board.

From a distance one might think that the Iraq war affects all Americans. But during my time travelling in Bush country, it was clear that the vast majority are not touched by it at all. Out of almost three hundred million people, fewer than one million have had to serve, either at home or abroad, since September 11th. It is their families who must say goodbye and do the worrying, wondering if they will be the next ones to die. Everyone else, I found, just went about their business as normal. Apart from showing support for the troops in small ways, the vast majority of Americans are not asked to sacrifice anything. They are not being asked to accept lower wages or work three hours a week to help the war effort. This is a different war to previous ones and, though most Americans accept that it is being fought in part for their own protection, they have been shielded from the worst of it.

The controls the administration places on news coverage means that the thousands of troops injured in combat are rarely seen and the flag-draped coffins of the dead returning are kept safely away from prying cameras. The media has done little to change this, somehow believing it to be unpatriotic to show the raw side of conflict. Out of every one hundred Americans, ninety-five could, if they wished, just go about their lives as if there was no war on at all.

The day the new plebes arrived in Annapolis, seventeen soldiers were killed. Their helicopter was shot down as they tried to rescue some special operations troops captured by the enemy in Afghanistan. The word around the Academy was that some graduates might be among the dead. I listened out for news of them over the coming weeks, but there was nothing: no statement of condolence from the President, no coffins to be seen arriving back on US soil, no public funerals, no way for America to thank them for their sacrifice. Just silence.

"BY TAKING THIS OATH YOU ARE COMMITTING to something greater than yourselves: to the values and ideals of the greatest country in the history of the world — the United States of America." After a brief speech from the top man at the Naval Academy, the swearing-in for new recruits was done and dusted in less than ten minutes. They pledged to uphold freedom and defend the Constitution. Parents cheered and cried and then left. And so began plebe summer, eight weeks of boot camp designed to separate the sheep from the goats, to toss out the misfits and the messers, and get on with the business of training the next generation of military leaders, a ritual that had been going on behind these walls since 1845.

"FORMATION!"

"Yes, sir!"

"Now!"

Weeks later I heard them march past the Bachelor Officers' Quarters at seven in the morning. They had a chant going, some of which I could make out from my front door: "The sergeant sends me off to chow, but I don't eat it anyhow. Left, left, left . . ."

There is no doubt that the war on terror has put large numbers of Americans off military service. Talk of a possible draft now permeates most conversations about how the country can stay ahead of the game. The US military has been designed to fight two wars at any one time and with a heavy presence in both Iraq and Afghanistan, everyone is wondering where the troops would come from to fight the next unexpected conflict or even to deal with the next unexpected emergency at home. Later in the summer, the delayed response to the devastation wrought on New Orleans by Hurricane Katrina led to accusations that members of the National Guard troops assigned to Iraq should have been on hand for the disaster.

The elite officer corps will always find recruits among the country's idealists and high achievers. Twelve thousand youngsters applied to the Naval Academy in 2005. To be even considered, they have to be top of their class, excel on the sports field and come highly recommended by their local senator. These are the Captains and Admirals of the future.

But re-enlistment rates in the regular army and navy have been falling off, causing the Pentagon to miss its recruitment targets. Inner-city kids, the rural poor and the National Guard now make up the majority of the boots on the ground. Middle-class youngsters I met in Virginia — a red, Republican state — didn't seem to have the Army high on their list of ambitions.

"Would nobody like to join the military?" I inquired of Scott, Aaron and Mike, all fourteen-year-olds who, if they did volunteer, could be on the frontlines four years from now.

"Yeah, maybe," said Scott, "but just to get college paid for."

"Same here," said Mike. College fees in America are now anywhere from fifteen thousand to fifty thousand dollars a year, making it attractive for many Americans to join up. Even factoring in the free education, though, the idea still held no appeal for Aaron. A shy six-footer with long hair falling into his eyes, he made it clear that he would be sticking with paintball, the military-style game where the opposing sides shoot one another with splats of paint. All three were ambiguous about the continuing war, concerned over how it was turning out, but still believing that it was about keeping America safe. Opinions on George Bush were vague and delivered with a shrug of the shoulder. "He's not all that bad," said Aaron. "He's trying to do what's right for us." While describing themselves as patriotic, they did not believe that meant having to fight for their country. Being patriotic was also about believing that America was right and strong and would not be brought to its knees by a bunch of suicide bombers, or by Bush-hating Europeans. Even at fourteen, they all knew that America's star had waned across the Atlantic.

"We have our problems. They have theirs. Let us solve ours and let them mind their own business," said Scott. The others nodded. None of the boys had ever been to Europe or anywhere outside of the US and there was not much curiosity about the world beyond Virginia.

"I'd like to visit another country, maybe some time later in my life," Scott said, pushing the boat out a bit, but not committing to anything.

THE FOUR LONG YEARS OF TRAINING and learning behind the walls of the Naval Academy finally do come to an end. On graduation day parents who dropped their children off as spotty youngsters return to see them transformed into young naval ensigns ready to lead. I heard that the graduating class of 2005 was to be sent on its way by the Commander-in-Chief, George W. Bush. I had not set eyes on him since the week of our interview so, at seven o'clock on a sunny Friday morning, I joined the long queues to get into the Navy football stadium in Annapolis for the graduation ceremony. Parents, grandparents, siblings and friends of the graduates had all made the journey from states like Illinois, Wisconsin, Nevada, Nebraska, Alabama and every other spot on the map you can imagine. Some of the graduates from the heart of America had never seen the ocean until they came to Annapolis; some didn't even know how to swim when they first arrived. Now the sea practically owned them. Families took their seats high up in the stands, fanning themselves to stay cool as the temperature climbed. Down on the football field, the class of 2005, nine hundred and seventy-six graduates, stood in rows, forming their own sea of dazzling white uniforms.

Almost everyone I spoke to was heading off for some further training before joining any battles. Most were going to flight school — some indeed lured by the high octane promise of the flying movie *Top Gun*.

"Tom Cruise may be to blame but I just want to fly," one graduate said.

"My dad flew, so it's a natural choice," said a female graduate.

"I'm going into intelligence." I finally found someone who wanted to keep his feet on the ground. However, he confided that the Navy wouldn't let him do anything else: he was colour-blind.

Only eight out of a class of almost one thousand were going into intelligence. So much, I thought, for the effort to shore up the faulty systems that had dogged the US over the previous five years. Several graduates were going off to join the Marines, a guaranteed route to the frontlines of war, while others were being assigned to ships and submarines. A thunderous roar of engines erupted above the stadium, and I immediately understood the preference for flying. Five slender F18 planes tore across the sky in formation at five hundred miles an hour. The last time I had seen these was at the NASCAR motor racing event in Richmond, Virginia. That seemed so far away from the Navy stadium in Annapolis but America is a place of so many brilliant images that it often feels like more than one country. "Oh, The Blue Angels!" gasped voices in the crowd, identifying the elite flying corps that graduates dream about joining. But only seven of the best pilots in America get to fly with the Angels at any one time. The rest of the *Top Gun* dreamers have to make do with bombing runs off the back of a ship.

The President arrived from DC in his helicopter, Marine One, and strode purposefully into the stadium to take his place amongst the assembled military leaders. He was surrounded by quite a selection of "chest candy" — current military slang for the colourful medals and ribbons that adorn the decorated officers. The last time the President had stood here was to award commissions to the class of 2001. Back then, no one knew there was a war to be fought. George Bush, however, may have been planning one. It has been suggested, on more than one occasion, that he had decided to take out Saddam Hussein well before the Al Qaeda terrorists launched their opening round of attacks on New York and Washington. The destruction of the Twin Towers may simply have been the excuse the administration needed to go after Iraq. According to the Project for the New American Century, a neo-conservative think tank in Washington, it was essential for America to reinforce its position as the world's superpower by spreading its values in the world's trouble-spots. Other more popular theories suggest that it needed to establish a foothold in an oil-rich part of the world. Then there was the old chestnut — that George Bush had plans to avenge a plot by Saddam Hussein to kill George Bush Sr. If he was even starting to regret his decision, it didn't show. Smiling at the crowd, George Bush looked as if he still had faith in himself and in his actions.

"When I spoke to the class of 2001, none of us imagined that a few months later we would suffer a devastating surprise attack on our homeland, or that our nation would be plunged into a global war unlike any we had known before. Today, we face brutal and determined enemies — men who celebrate murder, incite suicide and thirst for absolute power. These enemies will not be stopped by negotiations or concessions or appeals to reason. In this war there is only one option and that is victory." The graduates politely applauded.

"We are winning the war on terror," President Bush declared, outlining the number of Al Qaeda leaders put out of business. Brutal regimes in both Kabul and Baghdad, he added, were gone and their people liberated. The facts of the continuing unrest and carnage on the ground were not addressed that day. The enemies, he told those who would have to fight them, were terrorists, extremists engulfed by a hateful ideology. The clear message was that, no matter what their grievances, there would be no talking to them. The way to stop them was to destroy them.

Speaking to the nation as a whole, President Bush had found a way to sugarcoat the unpleasantness in Iraq and elsewhere. He did this with the reassurance that fighting the terrorists in their own backyards was a lot better that fighting them in American cities, and that the best way to honour America's lost soldiers was to finish the job. But for the people he would be sending to those distant and dangerous backyards, he needed something more. He needed toys, and he had lots of them. New technologies, he told the class of 2005, would be able to make them faster, more agile and more lethal. Aircraft taking off from the decks of aircraft carriers were now able to engage six hundred targets a day, up from two hundred in the first Gulf War. The new Hellfire missile was making it possible to take out enemy fighters on the middle floor of a building without blowing the entire structure to bits. George Bush promised advanced destroyers able to shoot down ballistic missiles, and submarines that could silently bring special operations forces to within striking distance of the enemy. Not only that, but huge floating bases would be developed at sea, bringing them even closer to the fighting. All this sounded as though it was still designed for a conventional war. Nothing he mentioned could stop suicide bombers in Baghdad or London or New York. But the President was clearly planning to stay on the offensive overseas. The defence industry would be kept busy.

To make things easier for military families, he promised to bring home troops stationed in areas outside the Middle East. But with the whole system stretched thin, he would have to keep reassigning soldiers to new tours of duty, and that was bad news for military families. Divorce rates have jumped since the start of the war on terror, with men and women being sent away for longer periods to places they could not take their families.

"We are getting married next Saturday," said Phil Haw, a newly commissioned naval officer, who introduced me to his young fiancée after the graduation ceremony. She was dark and fragile and looked about eighteen. She was not happy that he was going to be away but she would deal with it. Phil's mother was there too, nervous yet as proud as punch that both her boys had graduated from the Naval Academy. Phil, she was certain, would end up on some foreign battlefield. "We trusted God to get him this far; he is going to take him wherever he is supposed to go," she added, helping him to pin on his new insignia.

For two hours in the baking sun, the President stood and shook the hands of every one of the nine hundred and seventy-six graduates, posing for a picture with each one. It was clear that as Commander-in-Chief he was thankful for their sacrifice, thankful to have a thousand new potential leaders ready to do whatever he thought necessary. As a parting shot, he advised them to challenge established ways of thinking in their quest to defend America.

"The opponents of change are many and its champions are few but the champions of change are the ones who make history," he concluded as he handed them the blue folders containing their commissions.

GEORGE W. BUSH CLEARLY INTENDS to make history. Back in the White House, he had told me that history would judge him and suggested that I and others should hold off for now. In time, he believes, America's work in Afghanistan and Iraq will come to be seen as a turning point in the history of freedom. We have to hope that he may be right.

It had been a year since my own encounter with him. At the stadium, I couldn't get anywhere near Mr Bush without upsetting the Secret Service. In the year that had passed, more Americans had started to have doubts about his world vision and his actions. Others still felt that he knew what he was doing or were prepared to trust that he did. Most were following his progress on domestic issues. Some had just gone quiet on the subject of George Bush. No comment.

If I ever happen to be interviewing him again, I will ask if he had indeed planned to invade Iraq well before September 11th and, if so, I will ask him to tell me why. I will ask again if he really thinks the world is a safer place as a result of his actions abroad and I will still want to know if he thinks God is on his side.

Will I let him finish his answers?

I don't know.

And as for the small talk before the interview?

"How's your day been, Mr President?" I will ask.

And I'm sure that, as he straightens his tie, he will answer as he did the last time.

"Very busy."